"As coordinator of the Los Angeles Division's Employee Assistance Program (EAP), I found your book very useful in recently assisting one of our employees experiencing a problem with anger management. I am also considering showing your video presentation to our Peer Support group members to assist them in identifying employees that may need assistance with anger issues."

T. Sorrows
Special Agent/EAP Coordinator/Los Angles Office
Department of Justice/Federal Bureau of Investigation

"Dr. Barris' book is the best one I've yet seen an anger management. This book is "down to earth," with practical suggestions for change that are easy to implement. Barris successfully combines common sense with examples from his own life so the reader can identify with the concepts. I use Barris' book with my own anger management group and the majority of my clients have demonstrated remarkable growth and recovery utilizing Barris' ideas and recommendations."

Paul Susman, Ph.D.
Great Lakes Naval Base

"Having taught many anger management classes over the last four years, I have tried to buy and read every anger management workbook and see every anger management video that is available. However, I have been able to actually *use* none of the workbooks and none of the videos. The trick is to come up with a workbook that is simple, clear and focused on the reality that many angry people experience. I feel that Dr. Barris has accomplished this task in his book. I recommend this workbook for those who wish to master anger issues, as well as for those who conduct anger management classes."

Dan Melvor, Ph.D.
The Independent Practitioner:
Bulletin of the Psychologists in Independent Practice
A Division of the American Psychological Association
Summer 2001, Volume 21, Number 3

"I have been a drug and alcohol counselor for the past 24 years. A friend of mine gave me your book about three months ago and I fell in love with it. I use the book with my clients. They don't know what method I am using and they probably don't care. I do care, since it is important to me that they be responsible for their own feelings. I believe your book spells out how to do that in a way that speaks to the average human being. Thanks again for the great book!"

J. Johnson
Portland, OR

"Hi, Dr. Barris. My therapist has me reading your book *When Chicken Soup Isn't Enough.* I rejected it at first because self-help books bore me and, since I have extreme anxiety, I do not deal well with boredom. However, I must commend you on the writing style and the natural flow of this book. It is very easy to follow and relate to in a humanistic fashion. It really lets me take a look from the outside at my own actions and how I react to others.

"So part of this e-mail is to thank you for finally being a doctor who understands that the people who need self-help books are not always psychologists, doctors or in the psychiatric field. I also wanted to thank you for not having to plow through pages with tons of psycho mumbo jumbo that I know I can live without.

"Thank you so very much. My temperament thanks you. My blood pressure thanks you. My way of viewing others has changed and I don't feel like I am repressing any anger any more as a result of trying to manage it. Rather, I am totally starting to get rid of my control freak issues towards others and definitely taking my control back and turning it around on me as opposed to the rest of the world."

"Dear Dr. Barris, I wanted to let you know that I just finished reading your book *When Chicken Soup Isn't Enough* for the second time. It was suggested to me by my counselor whose help I sought after my wife of 16 years told me she was divorcing me.

"I've been trying to deal with anger all of my adult life (I'm 41). If I had read your book sooner, I believe I could have saved my marriage. The first time I picked it up it was like having the answers to all the questions through all of the years. I saw myself in those pages and found great comfort amidst all the pain and anguish I have caused myself.

"I've been able to use the gifts in your book to improve my outlook and day-to-day living since day one. I don't know how my story will end, but I know if I had created such a work I would want to know about its benefits. Your work has and will change my life forever. I will be a better person, parent, son, brother and friend because I have the knowledge and tools to control my thoughts. I strongly agree with your comments that there really is no healthy anger and no good use for it. Thank you."

2/19/02

To Bill:

Thank you for your wonderful friendship these past two years! Hope you enjoy the book.

Best wishes,

Brad

THE MIRACLE OF
LIVING WITHOUT ANGER

#2 IN THE *WHEN CHICKEN SOUP ISN'T ENOUGH* SERIES

Smiling Warthog Publishers

Reproduction or publication of the contents in any manner without the express written permission of the author is prohibited.

Barris & Associates, Inc.
5327 McKans Cove
Memphis, TN 38120

noangerdoc@aol.com
www.noangerdoc.com

First Edition

ISBN: 0-9711205-2-8

To my beautiful wife, Valerie,
whose love helped me finally see
that the only person holding me back
was me.

Thank you, my love.

CONTENTS

My mentor, Joe Becker, Ph.D., sat across the desk from me in his cramped corner office. With books and papers occupying every inch of space, it was hard to believe we could both fit. Joe's task this day was to bombard me with the types of questions I would need to answer as part of the graduate school interview process. His keen mind tracked every answer, inflection of my voice and movement of my eyes. As I left he made an observation that changed my life: "Brad, I don't know if you are aware of this or not, but oftentimes you come across as a pretty angry fellow. You might want to look at that." Momentarily frozen, I forced a smile across my face, thanked him for his time and observation, and then went about my business. But I never forgot what he said, because although it hurt like hell, he was right.

Since writing *When Chicken Soup Isn't Enough: Managing Your Anger in an Increasingly Angry World*, I have had the pleasure of speaking before more than 30,000 people on the topic of anger and, increasingly, the importance of developing emotional and behavioral self-mastery. Audiences have included mental health professionals, teachers, nurses, doctors, lawyers, police officers, business and lay people. I have traveled to major metropolitan areas and to small towns. But, no matter where I venture, people are seeking answers to help them deal with their own anger, the anger of a customer or co-worker, or the anger of someone they are struggling to love.

The original intent of this work was to revisit and revise the first book, taking into account what I have learned during the intervening two years. Those experiences, however, have taken me away from an approach emphasizing techniques for managing anger, to an understanding of anger on a deeper philosophical and perhaps even spiritual level. As this book evolved, concrete techniques for managing anger receded in importance, while understanding what needs to take place in order to let go of anger came to the fore. Those needs —including the importance of learning how to *transcend* our nature, how to acquire and accept the *truth*, and ultimately how to *let go* of anger—go beyond mere techniques into the realm of the personal philosophies by which we live. With these realizations I decided to abandon my efforts at revision and largely begin anew, this time with the title, *The Miracle of Living Without Anger.*

As one who has always enjoyed history, religion and philosophy I am amazed and disappointed by how little people know of these disciplines. I was speaking to a banker acquaintance one day. He was discussing the career plans he had for his son, currently in high school. Upon completing his secondary education, his son would attend a prestigious eastern university where he would study business and Mandarin Chinese since "the Chinese market will be larger than the U.S. market by 2035." Nowhere in the father's plan was there a mention of the son studying eastern philosophy, religion or history. How could the young man understand "the Chinese market" without understanding the culture underpinning that market? How can we understand ourselves, psychologically, unless we appreciate the historic, philosophical and religious currents that have led us to this place and time?

People who lack an appreciation for history, religion and philosophy delude themselves into believing that every concern or problem that passes through their minds must be new to the world because it is new to them. How childlike that view is! Those grounded in an appreciation of the three disciplines realize, however, that there really is nothing new under the sun. The problems we struggle with today—how to deal with our emotions, like anger, and behaviors, like aggression—have confronted humans for thousands of years. One of my hopes in writing this book is to reconnect present and future generations with the wisdom of previous generations regarding how to live life without anger.

For a human being to live completely without anger would, indeed, require a miracle. It is simply not possible. Even Jesus got angry. It is our nature, as human beings, to get angry. So why have I chosen a title suggesting that it is possible to live without anger? For two reasons. First, my hope is that you will view what I am asking of you as aspirational in nature. I want you to aspire to become the type of person you may not have believed yourself to be capable of. Second, by design this book is not for the weak of spirit. This book will be "in your face" for as long as you have the courage to read it. At each step of the way you will be challenged to think about your anger in ways that may, at first, seem confusing, strange and perhaps even frightening. I chose this title as a means of challenging you to go beyond your nature—to transcend your nature—and, in so doing, grant yourself a life where anger is, to the greatest extent possible, no longer an important feature.

I never intended to author a self-help book. Looking at other books in this genre I recognized that while many titles included words like "new" or "radical," most of what was being written involved the retelling of eternal truths. I marveled as hugely successful authors like M. Scott Peck, M.D. (*The Road Less Traveled*) and Stephen Covey, Ph.D. (*The Seven Habits of Highly Effective People*) poured "old wine into new skins" and then stood back as their books flew off the shelves. The enduring popularity of their books is a tribute to our thirst for the truth. The problem with both of these authors, however, is that while they do a wonderful job of telling you the truth, each fails to teach you how to *find* the truth for yourself. They have, in essence, given you the fish. This book goes the next step by teaching you how to fish for yourself. Like the works of Peck and Covey, this book is also about eternal truths—truths about anger—from which our generation has somehow become disconnected. My task is to get you started on a journey toward acquiring the truth and, along the way, to show you how it is possible to live without anger in your life. During the journey you will develop the skills necessary to complete the process on your own. There is an old saying, "When the student is ready, the teacher will appear." If you are ready, I am here to teach you.

A NOTE ABOUT THE WORDS OF WISDOM (WOW) BOXES

WOW BOX

Throughout the book you will come upon Words of Wisdom (WOW) sections containing the observations of the Greek philosopher Epictetus (Ep-ic-te-tus). Over 2,000 years ago he taught a philosophy that came to be known as Stoicism. Emphasizing moral obligation and self-control, Epictetus provided humans with a blueprint for leading richer, more fulfilling lives. Read his words with care. Savor them. Learn them well. Live them well. The truths of which he speaks are key to granting yourself the miracle of living without anger.

ACKNOWLEDGEMENTS

In the fall of 1972 I made perhaps the most important choice of my life when I decided to attend the University of Detroit High School. There my Jesuit mentors instilled in me the value of training in the classics, as well as the need to constantly challenge the assumptions by which we live our lives. I've never forgotten their sage counsel and, as you shall learn, this book is an extension of that questioning process. My love for, and gratitude to, those men who taught me so well are both profound and everlasting.

There are countless individuals who contributed, either directly or indirectly, to this book. One such person is Will Gordon, Ph.D., the founder of CorText Seminars. By allowing me to represent his organization throughout the country, he gave me a forum for developing my particular approach to dealing with anger. He also provided me with an opportunity to meet thousands of professionals who pointed me in the direction of writing this new book.

I also want to acknowledge the kindness of my personal assistant, Jeana Lightfoot. Travelling cross-country with me, even under the best of circumstances, is no easy task. In addition to living through my increasingly infrequent narcissistic outbursts, Jeana also served as a valuable source of new ideas. A keen student of the human condition, I value her wit and wisdom greatly.

Editorially and artistically I need to thank Elizabeth Walker, Jeff Joiner and Richard McCowen. Between working full time, caring for five children (including her husband Bill), and making the worlds best pesto, Elizabeth found time to edit my words into something more readable than anything I could have done on my own. Jeff and Richard, each a genius in his own way, handled front and back-cover design, and page layout, respectively. Oh to be so young and to have such remarkable talent!

One of the great pleasures of traveling is that I get to meet many exceptional people around the country. One such person is Claire McGoff. Having met at a seminar in Silver Spring, Maryland, Claire has taken the time to share with me her reactions to my books and seminars and, in the process, allowed me to see the world through her wonderfully perceptive eyes. Her suggestions are subtly woven throughout this book.

From the moment we met at a seminar in Los Angeles, the bond was destined to be a lasting one. To my wonderful friend, George Stanley, whose kindness extends to treating me like his own son, I want to acknowledge his help both professionally and personally. Someone once said that George walks around "collecting people." And so he does. Being added to his collection changed my life in ways I could never have anticipated. Thank you, George, for reminding me how important it is that we take care of ourselves so that we can touch the lives of others. You and Sally are blessings in my life.

Lastly, I would be remiss if I didn't acknowledge the faithfulness of our family yellow-labrador, Sweetie, who sat at my feet, staring out the office window, keeping me company for endless hours. Even now I hear her gentle snoring as she momentarily abdicates her responsibility to protect the family from all manner of evildoers. It is truly a dog's life!

To each of the above I express my most heartfelt gratitude.

CHAPTER ONE

WHERE DO YOUR EMOTIONS COME FROM?

To the degree that our emotions get in the way of or enhance our ability to think and plan, to pursue training for a distant goal, to solve problems and the like, they define the limits of our capacity to use our innate mental abilities, and so determine how we do in life.

Emotional Intelligence, *Daniel Goleman, Ph.D.*

A t the dawn of the new century, we are a nation of "emotion junkies." To "emote" or feel has become the *sine qua non*, or essential element, of what many believe it means to be human. A wife asks her husband, still in bed long after it is time for him to have left for work, why he remains at home. His response is always the same: "I don't *feel* like going to work today." The first question a doctor asks a patient or a therapist asks a client is, "How do you *feel* today?" People, even strangers, are constantly inquiring, "How is it going?" which is just another way of asking for you to report on your current feeling state. To talk about your feelings is a sign of emotional health; an inability to discuss your feelings indicates psychological problems. According to current psychological dogma, when you experience a loss you are *expected* to experience certain feelings. If you do not experience the required feelings—in the correct sequence, no less!—then something is wrong with you. The problem with this focus on emotions is that it has given us a world where many people are enslaved by their emotions.

*In addition to being enslaved by their emotions, most people lack the correct language for expressing their feelings. Emotions such as fear, shame, guilt, disgust, anger and sadness are always expressed in one word. If someone asks you how you feel, and you respond, "Well, I **feel** that people should honor their commitments"—"people should honor their commitments" is not a feeling; it is a thought or belief. While you may experience a feeling, like anger, when people don't honor their commitments, being able to distinguish between thoughts and feelings will be crucial to your understanding of this book.*

Certain assumptions underlie this focus on emotions. One assumption is that all emotions are essentially good or, at a minimum, neutral. Believing that all emotions are neutral or benign is not only untrue, but also dangerous. To equate depression with sadness about the loss of a cherished relationship is a recipe for potential self-destruction. To equate high levels of anxiety with appropriate levels of concern about the possible loss of a job is to freeze yourself in place at precisely the moment when you most need to be adaptable. To equate anger with irritation about a child's failure to return home on time is an error ripe with the potential for interpersonal conflict and hurt feelings.

The truth is that some emotions are helpful and others are not. Some emotions motivate us to deal more effectively with problems in our lives while others interfere with those efforts. Some emotions enhance our relationships while others wreak havoc. One of my tasks in this book is to teach you how to create emotions that are helpful and how to avoid creating emotions, like anger, that interfere with your living successfully. In all likelihood you've never viewed emotions as experiences you could learn how to create on demand. By the end of this book, however, you will be able to do just that.

Anger, sadness, fear, joy, love, surprise, disgust and shame are the eight basic human emotions. Research and my clinical experience indicate that anger is the most difficult of all human emotions to deal with—even more difficult than love! Before focusing on anger, it makes sense to discuss emotions more generally, moving toward the most basic question of all, "Where do my emotions come from?" Correctly answering this question is crucial to your psychological well-being and interpersonal effectiveness. Until you have a framework for understanding where emotions like anger come from, you cannot understand the theory that allows you to create helpful emotions and avoid creating unhelpful ones.

Your 10 year-old daughter comes home from school. Immediately you recognize that she is upset. She says, "Mom, I got so angry at school today! Where does my anger come from?" How would you answer her question?

When I present this scenario to people attending my seminars, I get illuminating responses. Four out of five women I ask this question of respond immediately, "Her anger comes from her father!" and the audience laughs. When things calm down and I press the question, a look of complete bewilderment spreads across the face of the person I have queried. After a moment, the individual usually responds, "Well, I would ask her what happened at school today." The implication being that it was what happened at school during the day that *caused* the girl's anger.

Think about that response for a moment. As long as the parent assumes that an event at school caused her anger, can the young girl ever learn how to let go of her anger? The answer, obviously, is "no." If an event caused her anger, and the event was something over which the girl had no control, then there is no way for her to respond other than angrily.

A failure to understand the source of emotions is linked to many psychological difficulties, including an inability to let go of anger. A saying in physics states that, "Nature abhors a vacuum." In the natural world, a vacuum or "nothingness" cannot be tolerated, so some physical presence rushes in to fill that empty space. Your mind works in similar ways. When you experience a powerful physiological, psychological, behavioral and emotional experience like anger, and you have never been educated about the origins of your emotions, you fill the vacuum created by the question, "Where do my emotions come from?" with the answer: "My emotions must be reactions to events in my life."

From this perspective, anger becomes something that happens to you and is viewed as a reaction outside of your control. Viewing emotions as reactions to external events over which you have no control renders you powerless in the presence of your emotions. This common belief makes you a slave of your emotions. This book is dedicated to disproving the idea that emotions are things that just happen to you.

As part of my workshops I frequently ask a member of the audience to contemplate the following hypothetical situation. Two sisters are playing with a doll in the backyard. All of a sudden the older sister begins ripping the doll apart until all that remains is a torso, which she procedes to throw into the neighbor's backyard. The younger sister runs into the house, upset and crying, and says to her mother, "Mom, Cindy makes me so mad when she destroys my toys!"

The scenarios I ask the audience to consider are as follows: Scenario 1—The mother says to her daughter, "You know, sweetheart, Cindy would make me angry if she did something like that to one of my possessions." Or Scenario 2—The mother sits her daughter down and says, "Wait a second, honey, you know it's not what Cindy did that *made you angry; it's how you **chose** to think about what she did that made you mad."*

Which scenario occurred at your house? Obviously, the answer is Scenario 1. We all grew up believing that other people or events were the cause of our anger because that's what the world believed and taught us.

If emotions are not things that just happen to us, then what are they? If what we traditionally believe about the origins of our emotions is wrong, then what is right? To understand where your emotions come from, you must first understand some of the basics concerning how your brain has developed and how it processes encounters with the world. An excellent discussion of how various brain structures influence the formulation of emotions is contained in Daniel Goleman's book *Emotional Intelligence*, and it is to a discussion of the material he presents that we now turn our attention.

The brains of *Homo sapiens* (the "**thinking** species") have developed through the millennia. The first parts of our brain to form were those structures associated with the brainstem. The brainstem is responsible for maintaining basic life functions, including heart rate, metabolism, respiration and stereotypical responses. As Goleman points out, "This primitive brain cannot be said to think or learn; rather, it is a set of preprogrammed regulators that keep the body running as it should and reacting in a way that ensures survival."

With the passage of time, the limbic system, or emotional brain, developed out of the primitive brain. Whereas the primitive brain was incapable of learning, the limbic system, because it possessed the capability to record or memorize experience, could now exhibit learning. The limbic system became the site of the Fight, Freeze or Flight

System (FFFS). The FFFS is genetically "hard wired" into each of us and its activation of the Sympathetic Nervous System (SNS) allows us to respond, almost instantaneously, by mobilizing our emotional, cognitive, behavioral and physical resources in order to protect ourselves from threats to our physical integrity. When you fail to look both ways before crossing a street, step off the curb, sense a car coming quickly, and immediately retreat to the safety of the sidewalk, you can credit the FFFS for saving your life.

Regarding the production of emotions, especially fear and anger, new research points to the importance of one limbic system structure—the amygdala. Situated just above the brainstem, the amygdala (one on each side of the brain) is the repository for our emotions as well as our emotional memories. We will return to the amygdala in a moment.

Developing out of the structures of the limbic system was the neo-cortex or "new brain." The neo-cortex is the part of our brain that has developed most recently. It is the site of our abstract reasoning skills, problem solving, planning and higher executive processing. I think of the neo-cortex as the part of the brain that makes us distinctly human. Regarding emotions, the neo-cortex—in particular the pre-frontal cortex—modulate, or even alter, our emotional and behavioral responses.

HOW EMOTIONS ARE FORMED UNDER ORDINARY CONDITIONS:

Knowing basic brain architecture allows you to answer the question, "Where do my emotions come from?" Under ordinary conditions, the sequence of neurological events that go into the generation of emotions, and their behavioral expressions, involves the following process: an event occurs in your environment, the event is then encoded by one or more of your senses (taste, touch, smell, sight or sound). A sensory signal is transmitted to the thalamus, a part of your brain that serves as a sensory relay station. That signal is then sent to the neo-cortex, where it is processed. After being evaluated, the information is passed along to the amygdala, and finally an emotional and behavioral response is produced. The diagram below (Figure 1.1) shows how this process works.

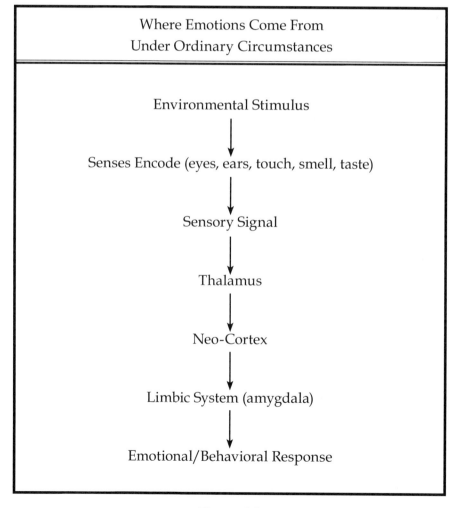

Figure 1.1

If I asked you to summarize this process, what would you say? Take a few minutes to ponder this question before reading further. What are the implications of this diagram?

If you said, "Something happens to me, I think about it, and then I experience certain feelings and engage in specific behaviors," you would be correct. It is crucial that you make the connection that, *under ordinary circumstances*, processing at the neo-cortex level (thought) comes before the formulation of your emotions and behaviors.

Why is it so important to understand this process? How many times have you said, "Well, I just got angry and said all those things. They were out of my mouth before I thought about them!" The implication is that your emotion (anger) and behavior (verbal aggression) preceded the thought process. What I am telling you is that, under almost all conditions, that is simply not true. In reality, you did think before experiencing anger and then behaving poorly. As you might expect, this argument about how your brain works, *under ordinary circumstances*, is crucial to understanding where you can intervene in the anger-producing process in order to let go of your anger.

You will have noticed that I emphasized the phrase *under ordinary circumstances*. While it is important to understand how your brain works to produce emotions and behaviors under normal circumstances, it is also important to understand how your brain responds under extraordinary circumstances.

HOW EMOTIONS ARE FORMED UNDER EXTRAORDINARY CONDITIONS:

Under *extraordinary circumstances*, such as a life or death situation, your brain is designed to respond almost immediately to protect you from harm. Under conditions of physical threat, the normal neurological process is altered: As before, an event occurs in the environment. One or more of your senses encodes that event. The sensory signal then goes to the thalamus. To this point everything is the same as in the first diagram. What happens next, however, is what Goleman refers to as an "emotional hijacking." Rather than the information going from the thalamus to your neo-cortex and then to the amygdala, the sensory information is "hijacked" and goes directly to the amygdala, after which an emotional and behavioral response is generated. The diagram below (Figure 1.2) represents how the process works.

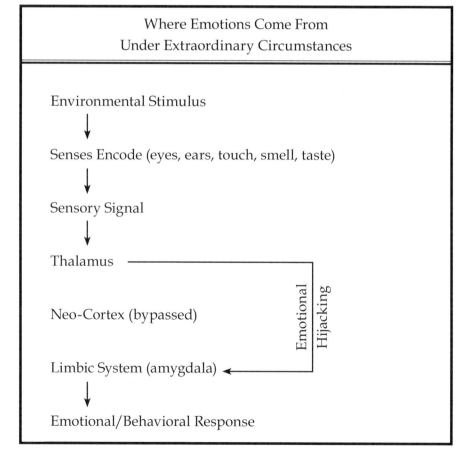

Figure 1.2

Under this scenario, the neo-cortex has been bypassed, with the information going directly to the amygdala. What are the implications of this emotional hijacking? It suggests that there may be instances in your life when processing sensory data via the neo-cortex may delay your response to the event. That delay can, under certain conditions, make the difference between life and death. In the example of stepping off a curb without looking both ways, only to realize that a car is fast approaching and may hit you, bypassing the neo-cortex and simply "reacting" by jumping onto the curb may save your life. Under these conditions, the "emotional hijacking" is really part of the Fight, Freeze or Flight System (FFFS) and can be helpful.

Now that you understand how emotions are formed under both ordinary and extraordinary circumstances, consider the following questions. When you leave the drive-through of your favorite hamburger restaurant, realize that you have received the wrong order and get angry, is that a case of emotional hijacking? Or imagine that someone says something you deem insulting, and you get angry; is that a case of emotional hijacking? Or assume you spend hours helping your child do homework, the child forgets to turn it on time, and you get angry; is that a case of emotional hijacking? I would hope that your answer to each of these questions would be a resounding "No!"

I make these points so you will see that you get angry far more often than you are confronted with life-and-death situations. Unless you live in a particularly threatening environment, have experienced some form of significant trauma or neurological insult, "emotional hijackings" occur infrequently in your life. My hope is that you will now operate from the assumption that your *thoughts precede your emotions and behaviors*. In the next chapter you will examine the nature and content of your anger-producing thoughts.

It was his last evening in the anger management group. When asked to summarize what he had learned, Ted announced, "The most important thing I learned in this class is that thoughts temper our emotions, and emotions temper our behaviors."

CHAPTER TWO

WHY IS LETTING GO
OF ANGER SO DIFFICULT?

Anger is the odd way in which we punish ourselves for the faults of others.
Seminar Participant, Albuquerque, New Mexico

L ike life itself, the process of letting go of anger is not easy. No one promised you it would be. There are many seeming "benefits" that prevent you from abandoning your anger. One such benefit angry people seem to believe in is that anger, at least in the short term, *works* for them. As they get angrier, and others give in to their demands, angry people make the mental connection that it was their anger that made others do what they had demanded. They actually believe that their anger has the power to make others do their bidding. Think about that notion for a moment. Does anger make other people do anything? Of course not. What really happens is that the object of your anger decides he or she no longer wish to experience the anger and chooses to give in to your angry demands. Unfortunately, angry people conveniently forget that others have freedom of choice, and they convince themselves that anger helped them achieve their goals.

In our home, my wife and I are like the characters from the movie The Odd Couple. *Val plays the role of the rather untidy Oscar, while I play the role of the neurotically clean Felix. Let's imagine that Val has agreed that her contribution to the maintenance of the house is that she will make the bed each morning.*

One morning she is heading off to work and I notice that the bed is unmade. I get very angry and scream, "Val, get in there and make that bed!" And she does! Did my anger make her make the bed? Absolutely not. She chose to no longer experience my anger and made the bed to "shut me up." The angry person, however, assumes that his anger makes other people do things.

Another seeming benefit of anger that makes it difficult to let go of is that it is "over learned." For many, anger has become the "default emotion." Just as the default setting returns the computer to its original state, anger appears to be the default emotional setting for most humans. Anger has become the emotion you get if you don't consciously choose something else.

If I asked you to tie your shoelace, and then asked whether or not you had thought about tying your shoelace, chances are you would say, "No, I just did it." But it wouldn't be possible to execute the series of hand, leg and foot maneuvers required to tie a shoelace unless instructions traveled from your brain to various parts of your body. The reason you would answer "no" is because the sequence of thoughts associated with tying your shoelace are over-learned or automatic.

I am proposing that a similar process is at work with your anger. Just as you have a manual or script in your head containing the instructions necessary to tie a shoe, you have a similar "anger script." Under certain conditions this well-rehearsed script gets activated and you become angry. Later in this book you will examine that script in considerable detail, understand the inter-relationships among its various elements, and then intervene in order to get an emotional outcome other than anger and a behavioral outcome other than aggression.

Letting go of anger seems difficult because anger helps some people hold on to the past, even an unpleasant past. Like other negative emotions such as clinical depression or excessive guilt, anger can keep us connected to people no longer in our lives. The story below illustrates my point.

For the final 10 years of her life, my maternal grandmother's nickname was "Grambo"—a conjunction of the words "grandmother" and the tough-as-nails movie character "Rambo" played by Sylvester Stallone. Grambo divorced her husband Charlie during the late 1930s—something unheard of at that time. Until her death in 1995, "That son of a bitch Charlie!" accompanied every negative experience she encountered.

I still recall her coming into our house one day after her car failed to start on a particularly cold winter day in Detroit. Her face creased with anger, she knocked the snow off of her shoes, slammed the door and announced, "That son of a bitch Charlie!" As if he were to blame for the car not starting! For more than 60 years she held on to her anger and, in so doing, kept their relationship alive. Though he died years before her, my grandmother's anger toward "that son of a bitch Charlie!" burned in her heart until her final breath.

Letting go of anger can be difficult because some people view anger as a more acceptable emotional response than feelings of hurt, grief, sadness, disappointment, guilt or shame. This is the notion of anger as a "secondary" or "blanket" emotion with other feelings—like hurt, grief, sadness, disappointment, guilt or shame—found beneath the blanket. When was the last time you heard a husband acknowledge to his male companions that he felt hurt, disappointed or sad about his wife leaving him for another man? Never! If anything, he would tell you exactly how angry he was about what his wife had done to him.

Based on my clinical work, whenever you experience anger in response to the disruption of a relationship you value (such as the death of a spouse or a divorce), your anger will almost always be of this secondary type. At some point our culture gave its seal of approval, especially to men, to use anger as a reasonable response to the disruption of an important relationship. But when you allow anger to dominate your response to the ending of a prized relationship, your anger compels you to act in ways that only deepen and prolong the loss. In those instances where anger is a secondary emotion, your task is to move beyond anger so that you can deal directly with your real emotional experience.

Letting go of anger is challenging because anger appears to be a universal, cross-cultural emotional experience. No matter where you go, you will find angry people. Some therapists, like Albert Ellis, Ph.D., the architect of Rational Emotive Behavior Therapy (REBT), suggest that humans are genetically predisposed to think in ways that produce negative emotions, of which anger is but one. Determining whether anger is a genetically determined response or a problem associated with one's upbringing is ultimately not important to this book; what is important is having you accept the reality that we all choose to experience anger at some point in our lives.

> *During my anger management seminars I often ask if there is anyone in the audience who has never gotten angry. Invariably someone will rather sheepishly raise his or her hand. I then respond, "Well, that's very interesting because if you look in the Bible even Jesus got angry on various occasions. If you are doing better than Jesus did, perhaps you and I can get together after the seminar to talk some more!"*

Research by Ray DiGiuseppe, Ph.D., and his colleagues, summarizing cross-cultural studies on anger, identified the following characteristics that make it difficult to abandon:

- Anger is experienced more frequently than the other basic emotions. During the course of the day, which emotion do you experience more often—anger, sadness, fear, enjoyment, love, surprise, disgust or shame? For many, anger is the emotion *du jour.*

- Anger is as intense as fear and includes high sympathetic nervous system arousal. With the activation of the sympathetic nervous system comes the release of adrenaline leading some people to report feeling "high" because of their anger. This is how anger can become addictive for certain people.

Willie, an anger management group member, observed, "You know, I've been addicted to everything. Alcohol, cocaine, you name it. I never realized that what I was really addicted to is my anger. When I get angry I feel good and, the thing is, I don't have to pay anything for it. It's free! And I can give myself a fix whenever I want it."

- Anger lasts longer than other emotional states. How long does it take you to cool down after getting angry? You don't have to be like Grambo, angry for more than 60 years, to know that once you get angry you tend to stay that way for an extended period of time.

- Anger produces a strong tendency to approach, rather than avoid, the person or situation your anger is directed toward. When you get angry, do you avoid people or "get up in their faces?" While some people get angry and retreat, most tend to move toward the person with whom they are angry. This may have something to do with the next characteristic of anger.

- Anger includes an experience of greater power or potency than other emotions. Anger transforms us into little Arnold Schwarzeneggers, all pumped up and powerful. One client reported feeling taller when he was angry! Since we perceive of ourselves as powerful when we're angry, it makes sense that we would want to confront the person our anger is directed toward.

- Fascinatingly, joy is the only emotion people are less likely to want to change than anger. Think about that statement for a moment. One can make a reasonable case for wanting to retain a state of joy for as long as possible. Other than joy, however, the emotion we most want to hold on to is anger.

Taken together, what do these characteristics of anger suggest? They suggest that the process of letting go of your anger means asking yourself to give up an emotion that:

- you believe makes other people do the things you demand of them.

- is over-learned or seemingly automatic.

- you may be using to hold on to past relationships.

- you may be using as a "mask" or "cover" for other feelings like hurt or sadness.

- you may experience more frequently than other emotions.

- you may be addicted to because of its high sympathetic nervous system arousal.

- makes you feel powerful and potent.

Given this formidable listing of anger's "benefits," is it really possible for anyone to let go of anger? Aren't the odds stacked against you? Since anger appears to be such a natural emotion, isn't asking that you abandon your anger the same as asking you to abandon your human nature?

Yes, the odds against letting go of your anger are indeed daunting; and you are right, asking you to abandon anger is asking that you set aside part of your nature as a human being. I am very aware of what I am asking you to do. And yet, despite the odds, many people, just like you, *do* let go of their anger. Why? Because, despite all the seeming benefits that accompany anger, there are also painful costs to be considered. Those costs are captured under the heading of "anger's bitter truths."

Anger's Bitter Truths

Could I, or anyone else, *force* you to abandon your anger? The answer is "no." Later you will learn that much of anger is about trying to control others. If you sensed that others were demanding that you let go of your anger, you would do everything in your power to resist those demands. Our nature is to resist the efforts of others to control us. In reality, no one can make anyone do anything.

I never argue with clients who choose to retain their anger. To do so would represent an effort on my part to control them and I am categorically opposed to that stance. My approach throughout this book will be to issue you an invitation to change. Once you consider the consequences attached to your continued anger, the decision of whether or not to change is up to you. Underlying this invitation approach is a profound respect for the right of each person to make decisions concerning the course of their lives—even decisions that will probably result in negative outcomes. So, while I can reasonably expect that one or more of these bitter truths will be visited upon you unless you abandon your anger, I still respect your choice *not* to give up being angry.

> *Each of us is free to choose whichever path we want to take in life. We are just not free to avoid the consequences of that choice.*

One of anger's bitter truths is that, eventually, it will kill you. Anger can kill you slowly, or it can do the job more quickly. Research data overwhelmingly indicate that anger increases your vulnerability to a variety of illnesses including stroke, cancer and diabetes, compromises your immune system, increases the lipid (fat) levels in your blood, makes it more difficult for you to adjust to and tolerate pain, and increases your risk of dying from cardiovascular disease. In this way, anger erodes your health and winds up killing you gradually.

> *When I go to our family physician for my annual physical, he always inquires about the status of my blood pressure. Since I began practicing the techniques for letting go of my own anger that I will be teaching you, my answer has always been the same, "Thanks for asking, Greg, but I don't have high blood pressure. I am a carrier. I give it to other people." Better that others should have high blood pressure than that you should.*

Anger can also kill you quickly. In high school I was notorious for my aggressive driving. One of my favorite tactics involved driving at night until someone got behind me with their high-beams on.

Certainly such a transgression couldn't go unpunished! I would slow down, wait for the offending vehicle to pass, and then "open up" on the driver (as if I were shooting him or her) with a specially installed bank of driving lights purloined from the landing gear of a jet aircraft. When I told my mother about this behavior, she responded, "You know, Brad, one of these days you're going to do that to someone and they're going to pull up next to you and put a bullet in your head. I know you think you're invincible, but you're not." Aggression begets aggression. In a world where people frequently carry weapons, aggressive behaviors can cost you your life in the blink of an eye.

Another bitter truth is that society will punish you for becoming angry and then behaving aggressively toward others. In his commentary on the poem "There Was A Little Girl" from *The Book of Virtues*, William J. Bennett makes the following observation:

> *[In the poem] we meet the child who, like most, is sometimes well behaved and sometimes not. And we face a hard, unavoidable fact of life: if we cannot control our own behavior, eventually someone will come and control it for us in a way we probably will not like.*

If you are unable to manage your anger and the aggressive behaviors growing out of that anger, society, through its legal mechanisms, will attempt to control your anger for you. Most likely you will not like the way this is done. The batterer intervention groups I conduct are filled with people who are being punished by society for their anger and for the aggressive behaviors that have sprung from that anger. No matter how justified you believe your anger to be, society will punish you, especially if your anger turns into aggression.

A third unpleasant truth about anger is that it destroys your ability to solve the problems life throws your way. As anger escalates, problem-solving skills diminish. Your own experience should validate this interaction. When you cut through all the psychobabble, life is basically a series of problems you need to solve. I do not say that discouragingly—I say it honestly and with hope. If life really is a series of problems, then it makes sense that the people who are effective problem solvers are likely to be very successful in the world.

What makes someone an effective problem solver? In addition to being good at acquiring and analyzing information, effective problem solvers learn how to *create* emotions that aid their problem-solving efforts and learn how to *avoid creating* emotions like anger that hinder their problem-solving efforts. Re-read the last sentence and let it soak in for a moment. What word in that sentence strikes you as being odd or unexpected? The word *creates*. As we touched upon briefly in the previous chapter, you can teach yourself how to create emotions that support problem solving, all the while avoiding emotions, like anger, that hinder that process. In the next chapter you will learn the method for creating emotions.

> The bumper sticker reads, "He who dies with the most toys, wins."
> I think it should read, "He or she who solves the most problems wins."

A fourth bitter truth associated with anger is that *life* will find ways to punish you for being angry. What do I mean when I say that life punishes you for being angry? Go beyond the notions of society punishing you, anger destroying your health and anger compromising your ability to deal with problems. You need to go deeper, to a more philosophical or even existential level, to find this answer. How does life punish you for your anger?

This is the notion of *karma*, "what goes round comes round," or "you reap that which you sow." How many opportunities have passed you by because of your anger? How many doors have slammed shut, despite your superior skills or knowledge, because others feared exposure to your excessive anger? Mysteriously or not, life has a way of evening the score with angry people because angry people always give life the means by which they are ultimately humbled.

> *My assistant, Kim, entered the office and began yelling almost immediately. The object of her wrath was Pam, one of the senior nurses at our hospital, and a woman notorious for her anger and trouble-making ways. "I hate Pam!" Kim exclaimed. "She is in nursing and we are in psychology. She should just keep her nose out of our business!" After listening to her tirade for a few minutes I settled back in my chair and, since I have not only attained Buddha-like physical proportions, but I would also like to believe some Buddha-like wisdom, I asked Kim to consider the following: "Why are you expending all this time and energy upsetting yourself over what Pam does? Why don't you sit back and let life take care of her?"*

> *Like most people, Kim was not immediately satisfied with this answer for two reasons. First, she wanted to see Pam get her "come-uppance," and she wanted it to happen now! Second, and perhaps even more importantly, Kim wanted to believe that she had a hand in Pam getting her "come-uppance" now! Trust me, when you let life take care of angry people, life devises punishments for them infinitely more delicious and exquisite than anything you can dream-up! You just need to sit back and let it happen.*

Anger's most bitter truth is that eventually it destroys your most important relationships—including the one you have with yourself. I think of anger as a "scorched-earth" emotion destroying everyone and everything in its path. If you are in a relationship with someone, and you want to be *out* of that relationship, my prescription to you would always be the same: go home, get angry and stay angry. If the other person is psychologically well adjusted, he or she will be gone in the blink of an eye.

Don't kid yourself; no one enjoys being around you when you are angry. Anger pushes others away, isolating you from them and from the world. Just ask your ex-wife or husband, or that ex-employer. Just ask your son or daughter who avoids your touch and nervously declines your invitation to join in opening Christmas presents. Unless you do something about your anger, you are likely to live life alone—and that prospect should scare you to death!

Even if you were able to tolerate living by yourself because everyone else had fled your presence, ultimately you still have to live in your own skin—you still have to live with yourself. The relationship we have with ourselves provides the foundation upon which we build relationships with others. If anger destroys that most personal of relationships—the one you have with yourself—then there really is nowhere else to turn. Like the proverbial house of cards that has collapsed, there is only the deepest of despairs.

> *One client, while discussing how anger had destroyed his relationships with his wife and children, observed that it had also destroyed his relationship with himself. "You know, Brad, I hate the person I have become because of my anger," he said. "I don't even really know who I am anymore, except that I am one very angry person."*

Lies You Tell Yourself To Justify Your Anger

Most people resist change. Chances are that you are no different. Going from the familiar stance of anger to the unfamiliar position of letting go of anger is a monumental change. Discussing the bitter truths associated with anger shows you the consequences of *not* changing. Once those bitter truths have been discussed, will you necessarily embrace change? Perhaps. Perhaps not. Like most people, you have probably mastered a variety of lies that you can tell yourself and others to justify your anger and to avoid the discomfort of having to change. Some of those lies might include the following:

LIE #1

"Anger is natural. Why would you ask me to abandon an emotion that is natural for human beings to experience?"

The belief that anger is natural is one I never argue with because it is true. For most people, anger has become the default emotional experience. While it may be natural for you to get angry, you are also capable of going beyond, or *transcending*, your nature. To illustrate the point that we are not captives of our nature, I pick someone from the audience and ask them the following questions:

BPB: "Excuse me sir, what is your name?"

Tom: "My name is Tom."

BPB: "Tom, would you mind if I asked you some semi-personal questions?" (Nervous laughter from Tom.)

Tom: "Sure, go ahead."

BPB: "Tom, do you poop in your pants?" (More nervous laughter.)

Tom: "Well, no, I don't."

BPB: "Great Tom, neither do I. When you were about a year old did you poop in your pants?"

Tom: "Yes I did."

BPB: "Fascinating; me too. Tom, was it **natural** for you to poop in your pants when you were a year old?"

Tom: "Absolutely."

BPB: "Wow, this is spooky! Now, let me see if I've got this right. When you and I were a year old it was **natural** for us to poop in our pants. Now that we are a bit older, neither you nor I poop in our pants. That suggests to me that both you and I, at least with regards to this biological function, were able to go beyond, or transcend, what was once natural for us."

Even though this example deals with a biological process, the analogy holds true regarding psychological phenomena. Recall our earlier discussion of how emotions are formed. We agreed that under almost all conditions thought precedes emotions and behaviors. The part of your brain that processes events, the neo-cortex, is the part of your brain that also allows you to transcend your natural tendency to anger yourself. You are not a prisoner of your nature! You do not need to be a prisoner of your emotions. You can master your emotions, like anger, and place them in your service.

LIE #2:

"I just get angry. Emotions are things
over which I have no control."

The idea that you can actually choose your emotional response in a given situation at first sounds strange. Throughout your life you have been taught that emotions are things that happen to you and are outside of your control. Nothing, however, could be further from the truth. You are learning that thoughts drive your emotions and that emotions drive your behaviors. In almost all instances, emotions are products of how you *think* in specific situations.

If you still don't believe me try, right now, to make yourself depressed. What would you have to do in order to feel depressed? My guess is that you would begin by generating a series of thoughts surrounding how bad your life circumstance was, how little control you had over changing that circumstance, and how things seemed pretty hopeless. As you came to believe these thoughts more completely, I predict that your feeling of depression would deepen. In this case, what caused your depression? Your thoughts. If you can learn how to control your thinking, you can control your emotions.

Not surprisingly, I have become adept at managing my emotions. Though this may seem strange, when I am confronted with a problem the first question I ask myself is, "What emotion would it be helpful for me to experience in order to solve this problem?" When I determine the emotion that would be most helpful, whether it be irritation, sadness, lower levels of frustration, or appropriate concern, I then create that emotion by producing the types of thoughts I know support that emotion. In this way I always have the correct emotion to help me deal with a given problem. Try it—it works!

LIE #3:

*"Only by expressing my anger am I going to feel better.
I should never keep my anger bottled up!"*

People sense that the world we live in today is an angrier place than it was in the past. Many have speculated about why that is the case, and almost all of that guesswork is wrong. The current favorite explanation seems to be that we live a world with too much stress and that excessive stress is causing all the anger. Our schedules are too rushed. There is too much traffic. We work too many hours. The implication is that if we could rid the world of stress, anger would go away. Poppycock! Yet this is exactly the type of simplistic explanation our culture craves because it views anger as a response to external factors, rather than a product of internal psychological factors.

An entire industry has been created to show people how to reduce stress in their lives. But, let's assume for a moment that you could eliminate stress completely. Do you really believe that you would never again experience anger? Of course not. That's because the notion of stress causing anger is nonsense. The stress-anxiety connection is not the only myth that psychology has given the world. As you will read below, the notion that keeping anger "in" is "bad" is another unhelpful suggestion popular psychology has advanced.

As I write this book, I have just celebrated my 44th birthday. Growing up during the 1960s and 70s, I heard pop psychologists declare that the worst thing one could do with anger was to "stuff it," "repress it" or "suppress it." Even during my clinical training in the mid-80s and early-90s, one of my supervisors warned a group therapy patient that the worst thing she could do was "gunny-sack" her anger.

Because of what I heard, I grew up with an unusual mental image of the dangers associated with keeping anger to myself: Like steam in a covered pot, my anger would cause pressure to build in my head until eventually my skull began to expand. Once the natural limits of expansion had been reached, my head would slowly begin turning just like what happened to the young girl in the movie *The Exorcist*. Gaining speed and momentum, my head would finally separate from my shoulders and launch into space like a satellite—all because I had kept my anger in! Don't keep your anger in—your head will explode! Or maybe not? Believing that the worst thing you can do with anger is to keep it in also means believing that the best thing you can do with anger is to let it out. Welcome, then, to the world where we all "let it out!" Not a very pleasant world is it? It does, however, provide one reason why the world is an angrier place to live in today.

While chronically angry people are more likely to experience certain physical problems than their non-chronically angry counterparts, that doesn't mean that the solution to your problem involves spewing anger out every time you experience it. There are countless examples of situations where keeping anger to yourself is precisely the right thing to do. There are also persons you are better *not* expressing anger toward.

> *At this point in my seminars I ask those in the audience who believe that keeping anger in is* **bad** *to try this simple experiment. A police officer is writing you a ticket for going one mile an hour over the speed limit. You anger yourself and recall that keeping anger in could result in your head exploding. What do you do?*
>
> *"Hey officer, how the hell can you give me a ticket for going a stinking mile an hour over the speed limit? Why aren't you out catching the real criminals instead of hassling the law abiding citizens who pay your salary? Better yet, I watch all these cop shows on TV and all you guys do is eat donuts all day long. Why aren't you at Artie's Donuts stuffing your big, fat face?"*
>
> *For persons trying this experiment I recommend always keeping a toothbrush, tube of toothpaste and a change of underwear in your glove box because chances are very good that* **you are going to jail!**

From this point on there will be no discussion of ways to keep anger "in," or how to constructively let it "out." This book is about learning how to *let go* of your anger.

LIE #4:

"There is such a thing as healthy anger."

I hear this often, even from colleagues who, because they were humans long before they became mental health professionals, are as reluctant as their clients to abandon a belief in the helpfulness of anger. The most compelling argument for the notion of anger as a helpful emotion takes this form: Anger can be viewed as a signal or a source of information. In this way anger alerts you to problems in your world that need to be solved. Used in this way, anger *can* be helpful and, in that respect, healthy.

The problem is that *no one* uses anger in this way. When was the last time you became angry and said to yourself, "I am angry. That must mean there is a problem in my life that needs to be solved." Never! Most people experience anger as I did in the example below.

I conducted a workshop for 200 professionals at a university-based medical school. In order to illustrate my contention that there is no such thing as healthy anger, I recounted the story of how I infuriated myself while writing my first book. Working under a deadline, I realized that all the changes I made to the manuscript for two days had gone unsaved by my computer. I recounted calling my wife, yelling at her about the situation, and experiencing the most intense desire imaginable to throw the phone through the computer monitor. After 20 minutes of ranting and raving, I recomposed myself and began addressing the problem of recovering my lost work. Where is the "healthy anger" in this situation? As in all cases of anger, it is nowhere to be found.

Since this is the way most people experience anger, I must respectfully disagree with my colleagues who believe in the notion of healthy anger. The idea that anger can be healthy or helpful is simply untrue. In order to understand why there is no such thing as healthy anger, you need to know how I define that term. Unfortunately, we won't get to the definition of anger until later in the chapter so you will have to continue upsetting yourself until then!

LIE #5:

"Hitting something, like a pillow, will
help me deal better with my anger."

This is the catharsis notion of dealing with anger. It emphasizes "letting off steam" as the best way to deal with the problem. Regretfully, there is no evidence to support the value of this approach. As a matter of fact, all the evidence supports that this is exactly the wrong way to let go of anger.

A perfect example of the foolishness of this approach is found in the movie Analyze This *starring Billy Crystal as a psychiatrist caring for his Mafia client played by Robert DeNiro. Crystal coaches DeNiro during an angry telephone exchange with one of his Mafia adversaries. When his coaching fails, Crystal suggests that he always feels less angry when he hits a pillow. Following his advice, DeNiro picks up a gun and unloads a clip into a nearby couch and pillow. "There's your (#!*a) pillow!" he snarls. Smiling nervously, Crystal asks, "Do you feel better now?" "Yeah," says DeNiro, "I do!"*

In the case of hitting a something, like a pillow, you *will* feel better immediately after discharging your anger. This is the same sense of relief people report after putting their fist through a wall or slamming a door. Unfortunately, rather than addressing the real source of their anger, they are simply rehearsing future aggressive acts. They recall the momentary relief they experience after behaving aggressively, and that split-second of relief reinforces the aggressive behavior. Not surprisingly, because of this reinforcement they tend to engage in more of these behaviors in the future. Countless studies indicate that people who use pillows or punching bags to relieve their anger actually escalate it and become more aggressive. Make no mistake about it, going from hitting an inanimate object like a pillow, to hitting another person, is not a big jump for many people. You can see how this technique may lead to significant new problems.

At the hospital, I met with a patient who had a long history of anger and aggression-related problems. To demonstrate his interest in working on these areas, he showed me some of the literature he had acquired at other psychiatric facilities. One document, titled "Physically Expressing Anger," contained the following pearls of wisdom for lessening anger: "Get in your car, roll up the windows, and scream as loudly as you can. If you don't have a car handy, take a pillow and scream into it. Do a shaking, stomping, primitive dance. Pound your anger into the ground. Get a drum and pound on it. Big drums are better because you can play them against your body, often between your knees, and their sound resonates deeper into you." Before I could offer my comments regarding these suggestions, the patient turned to me and said, "This is crazy! I've tried doing this stuff and it makes me even angrier!"

LIE #6

"If I don't get angry and behave aggressively, people will think I'm a wimp and walk all over me."

In our culture, few interpersonal styles are viewed as negatively as being labeled passive or a "wimp." American culture values tough, aggressive people, all the while scorning those viewed as "weak." You may get angry and then behave aggressively as a way to counter other's perceptions that you are weak. This approach has multiple problems. First, if someone is determined to view you as weak, all the anger and aggression you can generate will not necessarily change that person's view of you. As a friend in Alcoholics Anonymous once told me, "What other people think of you is none of your business."

Second, exactly what does the term "wimp" mean? Isn't a wimp, by definition, someone who is weak, out of control and ineffective? Ironically, the angrier you become, the weaker, more out of control and less effective you are. By becoming angry, you confirm what others already believe to be true about you.

Third, when you look at this whole idea of what constitutes real, authentic strength, isn't real strength where you are in control of yourself to the extent that you can actually choose your emotional and behavioral responses according to the situation, including responses other than anger and aggression? It takes no skill to get into a fight; it takes tremendous skill, personal strength and discipline to avoid conflict.

> *I am not a petite fellow — never have been. Despite my size, it is not uncommon for others to challenge me to fight. When I was younger, I accepted many of those challenges. The older I became, however, the more pleasure I derived from outwitting my nemeses. A friend once asked me to read Sun-tzu's,* The Art of War *and I never forgot these words: "To win 100 victories in 100 battles is not the highest skill. To subdue the enemy without fighting is the highest skill."*

LIE #7:

*"Even **you** would get angry if _____ happened to you!"*

Angry people use lies to avoid doing the psychological work necessary to free themselves of anger. With this lie they are desperately trying to recruit those around them to join in being angry by saying that, under certain circumstances, *anyone* would get angry. In the above example they fill in the blank with a situation most people would believe is the worst imaginable. When I am working with an angry client he or she will say, "But wait a minute, *even you* would get angry if you saw your wife being raped!" I'm sorry to disappoint you, but such would not be the case.

Anger so impairs your judgment, so diminishes your ability to solve problems, that it is *precisely* at moments like this that being able to discipline your emotional and behavioral responses becomes most important. Because I love and value my wife greatly, it would be crucial for me to respond in a manner that did not increase her chances of being further harmed. To be swept away by my emotions at such a moment would be to invite disaster. Can people be taught to respond this way? Absolutely. That's why we train law enforcement personnel in these techniques so they don't become embroiled in "The Arrest of Rodney King-II!"

LIE #8:

"I can't help it if other people or situations make me angry!"

Now comes the greatest lie of all. This lie is the source of more personal and interpersonal suffering than any other. It is the lie that everyone reading this book believes, as surely as they know that the sun rises in the east and sets in the west. All readers of this book believe this lie because it's what they have always been taught. It's what you believe because you live in a world where, if you experience something unpleasant, like anger, then someone or something else must be the cause of, or to blame for, your discomfort.

How many times have you said, "My mother makes me so angry!" or "I wouldn't have gotten angry if my co-worker had done what he said he would!" Do you see any problems with believing that other people make you angry? As long as you believe that other people make you angry, they are in control of your emotions and, by extension, your behaviors. As long as you believe that other people make you angry, you are powerless in the face of your anger!

33

> *People don't have the power to hurt you. Even if someone shouts abuse at you or strikes you, if you are insulted, it is always your choice to view what is happening to you as insulting or not. If someone irritates you, it is only your own response that is irritating you. Therefore, when anyone seems to be provoking you, remember that it is only your judgement of the incident that provokes you. Epictetus*

To exercise true personal power, to be in complete control of your emotional life, you must abandon the notion that others make you angry. Instead, understand that only you are powerful enough to create your anger. Accepting that you are the author of your anger is difficult because, among other things, it compels you to give up one of your favorite pastimes as a human—blaming others for how you feel and act.

If you truly understand what this book is about, the "blame game" stops now. Instead of pointing fingers at others, you will point them at yourself. Accepting personal responsibility for your own thoughts, feelings and behaviors is the cornerstone of self-discipline, true personal power, and is the necessary prerequisite for letting go of anger.

> *If it is our feelings about things that torment us rather than the things themselves, it follows that blaming others is silly. Therefore, when we suffer setbacks, disturbances or grief, let us never place the blame on others, but on our own attitudes. Epictetus*

THE ESSENTIAL ELEMENTS OF ANGER AND IRRITATION: TWO WORKING DEFINITIONS

Before defining the terms anger and irritation, let's briefly explore how we understand the world around us. Imagine asking two people to name an object with the following characteristics: a circular dial, at least two moveable pointing devices, and a series of numbers arrayed around the dial starting with 12 at the top and six on the bottom. Unless there were some form of serious neurological or psychological impairment, both parties would surely agree that the object being described is some form of time-measuring device like a watch or clock. There is consensual agreement among the parties that the watch is *real*. More importantly, the reality of the clock is not contingent upon who views it. In the real world, a clock is a clock. Period.

While there is an external reality that we can all reasonably agree on, there are also internal or "psychological realities" to consider. Psychological realities are contingent upon the person experiencing the event or object. This is why two people can experience the same event, yet have very different reactions. The reality of the event is not why their reactions differ. The differing reactions are based upon the fact that people perceive and interpret the same events differently. The mental filters through which we interpret events differently are our unique "personal philosophies."

A personal philosophy is the organized set of beliefs you have concerning how the world should be and how people you encounter in the world should behave. Initially, you acquire these beliefs through your interactions with your primary caregivers. As you became older, your beliefs tend to be influenced by a variety of sources including family, peers and the media. Your individual beliefs are woven together to form a coherent personal philosophy that guides your interactions with the world.

Is there a relationship between your beliefs about the world and anger? Absolutely. You will learn that anger is the emotion you experience when the individual beliefs that comprise your personal philosophy are *untrue*. Because the individual beliefs that make up your personal philosophy are untrue, your personal philosophy is also untrue. To the extent that your personal philosophy is built upon untruths, you establish the conditions for anger to govern your life. When your personal philosophy is congruent with what is real and true, you create the conditions for the production of more helpful emotional experiences. Thus, the process of letting go of your anger becomes a quest for developing a personal philosophy based upon what is real and true in the most profound sense.

If we are to talk about anger within the context of this book, we must agree upon a definition of this emotion that takes into account features common to all people. For the purposes of this book anger, from a psychological perspective, is defined as the emotion humans experience when:

- they live according to an untrue personal philosophy that is demanding and commanding. This philosophy emphasizes what the people believe they should or must get from the world or others.

- their personal philosophy emphasizes what they believe they are entitled to.

- their personal philosophy is starkly confronted by the realization that they cannot control others.

- someone violates one or more of the strongly held beliefs that make up their personal philosophy.

- the sympathetic nervous system is activated.

Accompanying anger is:

- an increased likelihood of aggressive behavior.

- seriously diminished problem-solving skills.

- less effective parenting skills.

- impaired relationships.

- an orientation towards the past.

- a resistance to change.

- a tendency towards embitterment.

Based on this definition, it's easy to understand why I disagree with colleagues and clients who argue that anger can be a "healthy" or positive emotional experience. From my perspective *anger is always unhealthy!*

It would be unfair of me to propose letting go of anger without suggesting another emotion to take its place. The emotion I am proposing you replace anger with is *irritation.**

For the purposes of this book, irritation is defined as the emotion humans experience when:

- they live according to a personal philosophy that is true. This philosophy is preferential in nature and emphasizes what people prefer, desire, hope, want or wish for from others and the world.

- they accept that, while they would prefer to be treated in favorable ways, they are not entitled to such treatment.

- they accept that, outside of their own thoughts, feelings and behaviors, they cannot control others or external circumstances.

- the sympathetic nervous system arousal is diminished.

---

*Therapist Note: There will be instances when you ask a client to go from feeling anger to feeling irritation and that term—irritation—will not feel right to either of you. An instance where this will be the case surrounds the issue of sexual abuse. Asking the client to go from feeling anger to irritation about the abuse doesn't come close to capturing their real emotional experience.

To date, I have been unable to devise an alternative term for irritation, and I leave it up to you to find one that fits for both you and your client. I will, however, point out that whatever term you and your client settle on for this emotional experience, it does need to include moving toward those elements that I assign to irritation: helping the client adopt a personal philosophy emphasizing preferences instead of demands; getting the client to accept that they cannot control others or external circumstances; orienting the client toward the present and future; helping the client be more open to change; facilitating the client's experience of gratitude; and helping the client become more assertive, along with improving their problem-solving, parenting and relationship skills.

Accompanying irritation is:

- an increased likelihood of assertive behavior.

- enhanced problem-solving skills.

- increased effectiveness in parenting children.

- more satisfying relationships.

- an orientation towards the present and future.

- an openness to change.

- a tendency toward gratitude.

Based on these definitions, letting go of anger involves learning how to move from anger to irritation. The importance of this shift, and how to accomplish it, are discussed in the next chapter.

You will not be punished for your anger.
You will be punished by your anger.

Buddha

CHAPTER THREE

Don't Always Believe What You Think: Learning How To Let Go Of Your Anger

Living upon a basis of unsatisfied demands, we were in a state of continual disturbance and frustration. Therefore, no peace was to be had unless we could find a means of reducing these demands. The difference between a demand and a simple request is plain to anyone.

Alcoholics Anonymous Twelve Steps and Twelve Traditions

In our culture people seek easy solutions to life's problems. Who wouldn't prefer taking a miracle pill to lose weight, rather than avoiding favorite foods and spending countless hours on health club treadmills? Well, when it comes to letting go of anger, people also look for a magic, effortless solution to distress. Unfortunately, no miracle pill or magic, effortless solution exists to the problem of excessive anger. Those hoping for such a simplistic solution need read no further.

While there are various ways to deal with anger, the overwhelming first choice of most people is to avoid the people or situations they believe make them mad. As you now know, the basic assumption that others make you angry is untrue. But, assuming that it were true, the problem with avoiding the people or situations you believe make you mad should be immediately clear. In the real world it is not always possible to avoid the people or situations you believe make you mad. You will get angry with bosses, spouses, children and in-laws. People will cut you off on the highway and co-workers will fail to complete projects on time. It is unrealistic to expect that you would quit a high-paying job, a long-standing marriage, driving a car or contacting your children and co-workers simply because you cannot control your anger toward them. To avoid these people completely, you would have to move to the Himalayas and live alone in a cave! Rather than avoiding these people, you need to change your angry response to them.

> *People with extreme anger problems believe that the only way they can deal with their problem is by isolating themselves from the rest of the world. Just as the agoraphobic isolates himself in order to avoid the anxiety associated with functioning in the outside world so, too, does the* **angeraphobic** *isolates himself in order to avoid encounters where he is sure to become angry.*

Other ways of dealing with anger focus on addressing the physiological dimensions of the problem. Countless books and programs have been written that emphasizing relaxation techniques and controlled breathing exercises as ways to reduce anger. While these approaches can be helpful and are covered in detail in my previous book, they fail to answer the question every angry person struggles with: "But why do I get so angry in the first place?"

Contrary to what some might have you believe, your anger is not the result of your mother toilet training you improperly; nor is it the consequence of her announcing on your 16th birthday that she will no longer breastfeed you! Understanding the origins of your anger does not require that you look into the murky recesses of a past you cannot change, nor toward others in the present over whom you have no control. Rather, the question, "But why do I get so angry in the first place?" is answered via the following proposition:

Life circumstances do not cause anger. Anger is a product of your faulty personal philosophy concerning life circumstances.

While the proposition itself seems straightforward, understanding the implications of this proposition, and then living according to those implications, is far more challenging.

UNDERSTANDING YOUR ANGER SCRIPT

When something happens, the only thing in your power is your attitude toward it: you can either accept it or resent it. What really frightens and dismays us are not external events themselves, but the way in which we think about them. It is not things that disturb us, but our interpretation of their significance. Epictetus

WOW BOX

In Chapter One, we touched on the notion that, just as there is a script in your head containing the instructions for retying a shoelace, so, too, is there a script in your head containing the instructions for producing anger. Now is the time for you to begin looking at the contents of that script to see how the various elements interact; and to see how you can alter the script to let go of your anger.

The psychologist Albert Ellis, Ph.D., has made several important contributions to our understanding of anger. One such contribution suggests that a particular type of personal philosophy is consistently associated with the production of anger.

The personal philosophy that results in anger takes life circumstances

we would *like, wish, hope* and *prefer* to have happen to us

and transforms them into

life circumstances we believe we *MUST, SHOULD, OUGHT TO, DEMAND* and are *ENTITLED TO* have happen to us.

In terms of understanding your anger, the key words to remember are "must," "should," "ought to," "entitled to," and "demand." When these words are present in the beliefs that make up your personal philosophy, they become part of a demanding and commanding stance toward life circumstances. Instead of preferring that life circumstances be a certain way, you now demand they be a certain way. When life circumstances do not unfold as you think they should, must and ought to, you make yourself very angry.

If you think about it carefully, however, *no person or thing, should, must,* or *ought to* be any way other than the way it is. Stop and ponder that statement for a moment because it contains a profound truth:

*No one, and no thing, **must** be any way – other than the way it is!*

Would your life be easier and more pleasant if life circumstances were exactly the way you thought they should be? Absolutely! But is that the real world? No, it isn't. For example, you may demand that your wife have dinner on the table when you get home from work. Would you be happier if she complied with your demand? Certainly. The important question to ask, though, is *must* she have dinner available the moment you set foot through the door? Obviously, the answer is "no." Living according to a demanding and commanding personal philosophy is a recipe for ongoing anger.

Dr. Denis, the dentist, came into the examination room to give my teeth one last check. His charming wife, Elaine, upon learning that my e-mail address is "noangerdoc," suggested half-playfully that her husband's be changed to "angerdoc." Upon learning of her suggestion, Denis replied, "I can't help it. I'm just a perfectionist. If only everyone in the world were just like me, I wouldn't have any problems!" Elaine (now his ex-wife) and I just smiled at one another.

THE ESSENTIAL NATURE OF YOUR BELIEFS

Humans possess a wide range of beliefs concerning themselves and the world around them. Those beliefs come from a variety of sources. Early on we adopt the beliefs of our primary caregivers, in most cases our parents. Because we lack the ability to critically evaluate those beliefs, we tend to adopt them "whole cloth," or in their entirety. Later in life we acquire beliefs from other sources including peers, teachers and the media. No matter how we acquire our beliefs, one fact remains constant: *Once we acquire a belief, it is automatically granted the status of truth.*

Think about it for a moment. Isn't the assumption that since you believe "X," that "X" (whatever "X" might be) must be true? Of course it is. Once granted the status of truth, you will argue for, defend against and, most importantly, never question your beliefs. When others hold beliefs in agreement with yours, they are correct and living according to what is true. When others hold beliefs at variance with yours, then they are wrong and must be converted to the truth—albeit your version of the truth!

This tendency to grant the status of truth to your beliefs plays an important role in the generation and perpetuation of anger. In order to let go of anger, you need to become very skilled at a process that is fundamentally unnatural for all human beings. That process involves actively examining and challenging your beliefs about life circumstances. Bearing that in mind, I assert the radical notion that:

*Whenever you are angry, your beliefs about life circumstances are **ALWAYS** untrue!*

If anger is based upon the untrue beliefs that make up your personal philosophy, then how do you find the truth and, in the process, let go of anger? That is your next task.

IN SEARCH OF THE TRUTH:
HOW TO REWRITE YOUR ANGER SCRIPT

As you learned in Chapter One, and contrary to what some would have you believe, anger rarely appears "out of the blue." Clients have described situations in which their anger appeared to come over them so quickly that it seemed almost like a panic attack, seizure or some other form of neurological event. They may have been reporting what we now know to be a form of "emotional hijacking." In most instances, however, a period of time occurs when you process a given event. It is during that processing or thinking stage that you need to intervene in order to let go of your anger.

In addition to helping us understand the type of personal philosophy that underpins anger (a demanding and commanding philosophy made up of beliefs full of shoulds, musts and oughts), Dr. Ellis also developed a technique that helps you unpack and examine your anger-producing script. Known as the *ABCs of REBT*, we will use this approach to help you understand the origins of your anger and how to let go of it.

According to the ABCs of REBT:

A = <u>A</u>ctivator: There are six important points to remember about activators:

- Activators are "what start something;" they are triggers, catalysts, stimuli, etc. for your anger.

- Activators do not cause your anger.

- Anyone or anything can serve as an activator for your anger.

- Activators are always problems in your life that need to be solved.

- You have 0% control over the activators in your life.

- Activators, in and of themselves, are meaningless.

B = <u>B</u>eliefs: There are seven important points to remember about anger-producing beliefs:

- The combination of your anger-producing beliefs makes up your demanding and commanding personal philosophy. This type of personal philosophy views the world in "black-and-white terms," and is rigid, dogmatic and inflexible.

- Anger-producing beliefs always include red-flag words like "should," "must" and "ought to."

- Beliefs are how you interpret, or what you think about, or the meanings you assign to, the activator.

- Beliefs can either be helpful or unhelpful for you, and

for your important relationships.

• Beliefs can either help you solve problems or make problems worse.

• Each of us can have different beliefs about the same activator.

• Unless you have serious psychological problems (such as schizophrenia), you exercise 100% control over your beliefs about a particular activator.

C = <u>Consequences:</u> These are the emotions (such as anger and irritation) you feel, the behaviors you engage in, and the physical responses you create for yourself when you hold certain beliefs about the activator:

• Behaviors associated with anger include throwing things around the house, cursing at your spouse and slamming the wall with your fist.

• Physical consequences associated with anger include muscles tensing, heart racing, blood pressure increasing and hands beginning to shake.

• When considering the emotional consequences it is helpful to imagine that there is an Internal Anger Scale inside your head. This scale (see Figure 3.1 on the next page) goes from 0, which is no anger, to 10, which is as intensely angry as you can get. The scale is divided into two ranges, 0-5 and 5-10. The name I have given to the emotion between 0-5 is irritation, while the name for the emotion between 5-10 is anger.

Behavioral Consequences   *Physical Consequences*

Behavioral Consequences		Scale		Physical Consequences
	A	10	A	Increased Blood Pressure
Serious Physical Aggression	N	9	N	Increased Heart Rate
Low-Level Physcial Aggression	G	8	G	Rapid, Shallow Breath
Threats/Verbal Aggression	E	7	E	Increased Muscle Tension
	R	6	R	Adrenaline Released
	I	5	I	
Personal Time Out	R	4	R	Trembling
	T	3	T	
Assertiveness	A	2	A	Flushed Face
	T	1	T	
	N	0	N	

Figure 3.1: Internal Anger Scale

Personal Philosophy	Emotion	Behaviors	Problem Solving	Parenting Skills	Relationships	Time Orientation	Change	Stance Towards Life
Demanding/ Commanding Beliefs	Anger	Aggression	Decreased	Punishment	Blaming	Past	Resistant	Embitterment
↓	↓	↓	↓	↓	↓	↓	↓	↓
Preferential Beliefs	Irritation	Assertion	Increased	Discipline	Personal Responsibility	Present/ Future	Open	Gratitude

Figure 3.2: Anger vs. Irritation

Letting go of anger is one of the greatest gifts you can give yourself and those around you. What makes it an even greater gift is that once you make the shift from anger to irritation, you position yourself to make important changes in other areas of your life. The diagram on the previous page (Figure 3.2) shows the changes you position yourself to make once you give up being angry.

This diagram (Figure 3.2), which assumes the formation of emotions under ordinary circumstances, illustrates the following important points:

- Under ordinary circumstances, thoughts precede emotions and behaviors.

- Under ordinary circumstances, emotions drive behavior.

- Emotions can support, or override, desired behaviors.

- Anger is associated with:
  - increased likelihood of aggressive behavior;
  - diminished problem-solving skills;
  - the use of punishment when trying to get children to alter their behavior;
  - impaired relationships;
  - an orientation toward the past;
  - a resistance to change; and,
  - a tendency toward embitterment.

- Shifting from anger to irritation positions you to:
  - behave assertively rather than aggressively;

- improve your problem-solving skills;

- rely on discipline rather than punishment when trying to get children to alter their behavior;

- improve your relationships;

- orient yourself toward the present and future;

- be more open to change; and,

- experience feelings of gratitude.

• Most psychological approaches try to eliminate specific undesirable behaviors, or teach specific desirable behaviors. This diagram suggests that *before* working on changing specific behaviors, you must work on changing the emotion, in this case anger, that is driving unhelpful responses or interfering with the production of helpful responses.

• Is it possible for you to engage in helpful behaviors (for example, assertion rather than aggression), even though you are *feeling* anger? The answer is "yes." In a case like this, however, there is a "disconnect" between your feelings and behaviors. This type of disconnect causes considerable distress over time. The best way to deal with this type of emotional/behavioral disconnect is to help you move from anger to irritation so that your emotions are congruent with, and supportive of, your desired behaviors.

Let's look at how moving from anger to irritation affects behaviors, problem solving, parenting and relationship skills via the following conversation with Bill:

51

BPB: "We've been talking about the need to have you move from anger to irritation. Let's spend a few minutes looking at why that shift in your emotions is so important. When you are angry, can we agree that you are much more likely to behave aggressively toward your family?"

BILL: "Yes."

BPB: "Does behaving that way toward your wife and kids cause you a lot of trouble?"

BILL: "Yes, it does."

BPB: "By moving from anger to irritation, you will be less likely to behave aggressively and more likely to behave assertively. Can we agree that, within the context of your family, assertive behavior is preferable to aggressive behavior?"

BILL: "Absolutely."

BPB: "Next, can we agree that, when you are angry, your ability to solve problems decreases? That you become a less-effective problem solver the angrier you get?"

BILL: "That's true."

BPB: "By moving from anger to irritation, your problem-solving skills will improve and you should get more of the good things you want from life."

BILL: " That makes sense."

BPB: "When you are angry, and trying to get your child to alter his behavior, what do you do?"

BILL: "When I'm angry, all I can think about is punishing my son."

BPB: "If you first let go of your anger, my suspicion is that you will be less likely to use punishment and more likely to use discipline. Is there a difference between punishment and discipline?"

BILL: "There's a big difference."

BPB: "Finally, let's talk about your marriage. When you are angry at your wife, what do you spend all of your time doing?"

BILL: "Well, I blame her a lot for my anger."

BPB: "If you gave up your anger what would happen?"

BILL: "I guess I'd have to take a hard look at myself."

BPB: "Do you think it would make a difference in your marriage if, instead of blaming your wife for your anger, you took responsibility for it yourself?"

BILL: "It would probably change everything between us."

BPB: "It might not change everything between the two of you but I'll tell you what it would do, it would open lines of communication that have been shut for years because of your anger."

MY CONVERSATION WITH AMY

During each seminar I ask someone from the audience to volunteer a situation, either in the recent or distant past, where they became angry as close to 10 on the Internal Anger Scale as possible. The volunteer comes to the front of the room and joins me in the process of unpacking their anger-producing script. By watching me work with a "client," members of the audience learn the skill themselves. What follows is my conversation with Amy*, an attractive woman in her early 30s. For the purposes of this example, assume that Amy already knows the ABCs of REBT.

BPB: "Thanks for volunteering, Amy. Shall we get started?"

Amy: "Sure."

BPB: "You already know about the ABCs, so let's start by looking at the activator. What happened that triggered your anger?"

Amy: "I overheard a conversation my husband was having with another woman. They were talking about meeting for dinner later that week. I also learned that they had been having an affair for six months."

BPB: "So your husband having an affair would be the activator, right?"

---

*Amy's story is a composite of many interactions I have had with seminar volunteers and actual clients over the years. Resemblance to any person, either living or deceased, is purely unintentional.

Amy: "That's right."

BPB: "As you overheard the conversation, how did you *feel* (emotional consequence)?"

Amy: "How do you think I felt? I was furious! At least a 9 or 10 on your Anger Scale."

BPB: "What did you *do* (behavioral consequence) when you learned that your husband was having an affair?"

Amy: "I followed him to the restaurant where they met for dinner and confronted them."

BPB: "What do you mean by confronting them?"

Amy: "I began yelling at my husband and demanding that he explain himself. Eventually I threw a glass of wine on him. I started screaming at the woman, calling her a whore and a home-wrecker. It got very ugly and eventually the manager asked me to leave."

BPB: "As all of this was going on, what kinds of changes did you notice taking place inside your *body* (physical consequences)?"

Amy: "My heart was racing. I remember that it seemed like I was going to pass out because I couldn't catch my breath. I was shaking all over. It was terrible!"

Based on this information, you can identify Amy's activator and the consequences she experienced.

> **Activator:** Husband having an affair.
>
> **Consequences:** Her emotional consequence is intense anger (a "9" or "10" on the Internal Anger Scale). She began yelling at her husband, threw a glass of wine on him, started screaming at the woman and got thrown out of the restaurant (behavioral consequences). Her heart was racing, she couldn't catch her breath and she was shaking all over (physical consequences).

At this point, Amy believes firmly in the *A $\xrightarrow{causes}$ C Connection.* This is the idea that other people, situations or life circumstances (activators) *caused* her anger.

> **BPB:** "Let me see if I understand this correctly. You are saying that your husband having an affair *made* you angry at the rate of a 9 or 10, which then caused you to confront them both, and led to your heart racing, being unable to catch your breath and shaking all over. Am I understanding you correctly?"
>
> **Amy:** "That's exactly what I am saying. He *made* me so mad!"

I now invite Amy to look at the relationship she has established in her mind between activators and consequences.

> **BPB:** "Amy, let's look at this connection you're making between what your husband did and how you responded. If it were true that he made you angry in this situation, who would be in control of you?"
>
> **Amy:** "Well, I guess he would be in control of me."

BPB: "What do you think about that? Do you like the idea that he is in control of you? Do you like the notion that your husband, who seems to have acted in a manner that violates some of your most important beliefs, is also now in control of your emotions and behaviors?"

Amy: "Of course not! I don't like that at all. I want to be in control of myself, but I don't know how to do that."

BPB: "I want you to be in control of yourself, too. To regain control of yourself we need to look more closely at the connection you've made in your mind that it was what your husband did that caused your anger. This is the idea that activators cause consequences. If it's true that activators cause consequences, then I want you to continue believing that he made you angry. If it's not true, I'm going to ask to give up believing in that connection. Fair enough?"

Amy: "Okay."

BPB: "Let's imagine that we go to the mall on a Saturday afternoon and pick out, at random, 100 women all of whom are married. Each woman learns that her husband is having an affair. You get my point? Instead of this situation being between just you and your husband, the same situation occurs, but now between 100 wives and their husbands."

Amy: "Okay, I get it. One hundred wives and husbands. All the husbands are having affairs."

BPB: "Now Amy, I need you to step back for a moment and look at this situation not through your anger, but *logically*. You are saying that your husband having an affair *caused* your anger. If that's true, then how many of the 100 wives, upon learning that their husbands were having affairs, would have to experience pretty much the same consequences you did?"

Amy: "Well, I guess most of the wives would respond the way I did."

BPB: "Amy, you're not answering my question. You are saying that your husband having an affair *made* you angry. If that's true, then, given the same activator, how many of those 100 wives would have to feel and behave like you did—*logically*?"

Amy: "Well, logically, they would *all* have to feel and behave the same way I guess."

BPB: "Right. If the activator causes these responses in you, then logically it would cause the same responses in everyone encountering it. Now, I want you to tell me *how likely* it would be that all 100 wives would experience the same reactions you did, given the same activator?

Amy: "Geeze, I don't know. But it would be a lot, I can tell you that."

BPB: "Maybe 50? Maybe 75? Let's assume for the sake of this discussion that 99 out of the 100 wives had the same reaction you did. And would you agree that the chances of 99 different women responding the same way you did would be pretty small?"

Amy: "Agreed."

BPB: "Even if 99 out of the 100 wives experienced the same reactions you did, that means *one did not.* And if even one wife does not experience the same responses you did, what does that mean about activators *causing* consequences? Is that true or false?"

Amy: "Well, when you look at it that way, it's false."

BPB: "So do activators cause anger?"

Amy: "I guess not."

BPB: "Does your husband *make* you mad when he has an affair?"

Amy: "No."

BPB: "Right. He doesn't make you mad. And if he doesn't make you mad, then who do you think is making you angry?"

Amy: "I guess it must be me."

BPB: "Another way of looking at this situation involves asking yourself how much control you have over what has happened. On a scale going from 0%, which is none, to 100%, which is complete or total, how much control do you have over your husband's decision to have an affair?"

Amy: "I don't have any control over his decision. If I did, he wouldn't have had the affair."

BPB: "Right. Now the question becomes, 'How much control do you have over *how you think* about your husband having an affair?' "

Amy: "I have total control over how I think about things."

BPB: "That's right Amy. So which is going to be a better use of your time? Trying to change your husband, over whom you have no control, or trying to change your thoughts about what your husband has done, over which you have total control?"

Amy: "The second one. Changing my thoughts."

At this point in the conversation certain people develop what I refer to as the "hairball syndrome." Hairballs are those obstructions animals, like cats, develop that cause them to emit a terrible choking sound at times. When you get to the point where you ask the person what is a better use of their time, trying to change the activator, over which or whom they have no control, or working on changing how they think about the activator, over which they have total control, they know the "correct" answer—it's just that they don't want to admit it. At these times they often respond with the same kind of choking sensation we see in animals that have something stuck in their throat. "Well, (cough, hack, wheeze) I guess it would be better (more coughing, hacking, wheezing) to work on changing (cough, cough, hack) how I think about (wheeze, hack) this situation."

An important series of beliefs underlay the hairball response, and you must identify and know how to deal with them. Can you figure them out? What could you say to yourself about the activator that would lead you to have this much difficulty responding to the question, "What's a better use of your time, trying to change the activator, over which or whom you have no control, or working on changing how you think about the activator, over which you have total control?"

Had Amy demonstrated the hairball syndrome, the underlying thoughts would have sounded like this: "Let me see if I have this correctly. I am paying you all this money to help me deal better with my anger toward my husband and you're saying that my husband having an affair is *not* what's making me angry—it's how I *think* about his having an affair that is making me angry? That I am angering myself? Why do *I* need to be the one who does all the hard work of changing my beliefs, when he is the no-good bastard who is cheating on me?" Stated more specifically, the belief is always, *"Why do I need to be the one to change when the other person is the one who has wronged me?"* The answer to the question is that the only way for her to get unstuck from her anger is for her to change what she can—which, in this case, is her thinking about what her husband has done. Let's return now to the example.

> **BPB:** "Excellent Amy! Now I need to ask you one last question. As long as you believe that your husband makes you angry, and you have no control over changing his behavior, where does that leave you with your anger?"

> **Amy:** "I'll tell you where it leaves me. It leaves me *stuck* being angry all the time and I am getting tired of being angry."

BPB: "I'm glad you're getting tired, Amy, because we need to get you 'unstuck' from all this anger. I'll show you how to do that right now."

Now that Amy has broken the *A $\xrightarrow[causes]{}$ C Connection* (the idea that her husband's affair *caused* her anger), her next task is to identify what is really causing her anger.

BPB: "Amy, do you remember what you thought when you learned that your husband was having an affair? What did you tell yourself? What went through your head?"

Amy: "I remember thinking, 'How could he do this to the kids and me? How could he betray me like this? I've honored my vow to be faithful to him, so he should honor his vow to be faithful to me!' "

BPB: "It sounds like you have some pretty strongly held beliefs about what your husband should and shouldn't do within the context of your marriage, agreed?"

Amy: "So what! Shouldn't people keep their promises to each other?"

BPB: "Before I answer that question, let me suggest something. One of the things we know about people who get angry is that they think in very specific ways. They have a personal philosophy made up of beliefs that include certain "red flag" words like should, must, ought to, has to, needs to, etc. These words become part of a demanding and commanding personal philosophy where, as in this case, you are making demands of, and issuing commands to, your husband. In your mind you are in essence demanding that he not do what he has already done. Do you see that?"

Amy: "I do now."

BPB: "In order to identify your anger-producing beliefs, we need to go back to what you told yourself about the affair and make a few small changes. Your first two thoughts about the affair were really questions that you asked yourself, 'How could he do this to the kids and me?' and 'How could he betray me like this?' In order to find the beliefs that are driving your anger, you need to change the questions you have asked yourself into statements. The statement form of, 'How could he do this to the kids and me?' is what?"

Amy: "He *shouldn't* do this to me and the kids!"

BPB: "Right. And the statement form of, 'How could he betray me like this?' is what?"

Amy: "He *shouldn't* betray me like this!"

BPB: "Now you've got it. The last anger-producing belief doesn't need to be changed into a statement. It's already in statement form. What was that last belief?"

Amy: "I've been faithful to him, so he *should* honor his vows and be faithful to me!"

BPB: "Amy, when you don't get what you demand of your husband, or when he doesn't do what you think he *should* or *ought to* do, how do you feel?"

Amy: "I guess I *make myself* very angry."

Amy can now make the connection between her demanding and commanding beliefs toward her husband and the production of her anger. Once this connection is clear, Amy needs help converting her anger into irritation—the process we know is necessary for her to let go of her anger. Letting go of anger requires that we guide her through the final parts of the ABCs—the D, E and F.

D = <u>Disputation:</u> There are five important points to remember when disputing anger-producing beliefs:

- Disputing, or challenging, anger-producing beliefs is the most difficult part of the process of letting go of anger.

- Challenging your anger-producing beliefs is unnatural because you assume that if you believe something, it must be true.

- This is where you transcend your nature by questioning the beliefs that make up your demanding and commanding personal philosophy.

- Questioning the beliefs that make up your demanding and commanding personal philosophy takes courage and the ability to ask yourself questions that sometimes lead to uncomfortable answers.

- The following are the major forms of disputation:

— "Where is it written that...?"

— "Does it follow that...?"

— "Does thinking this way help me or hurt me?"

— "Does thinking this way help or hurt my important relationships?"

— "Does thinking this way solve the problem posed by the activator?"

— "Would your best friend view the activator the same way you do?"

Remember to discriminate between events themselves and your interpretations of them. Remind yourself: "What hurts this person is not the occurrence itself, for another person might not feel oppressed by this situation at all. What is hurting this person is the response he or she uncritically adopted." Epictetus

BPB: "Amy, we agree that it is your thinking about your husband's behavior that is making you angry. Now we need to help you find a new way of thinking. Ultimately, the process of letting go of anger requires that you challenge your anger-producing beliefs to see whether or not they are *true*.

Remember how we discussed anger–producing beliefs as making up a faulty, demanding and commanding personal philosophy? From my perspective, the most powerful question you can ask yourself about your anger-producing beliefs is, 'Where is it written that...?' The reason why this question is more powerful than any of the others is that it is a profoundly philosophical question. This question forces you to step back and consider the world as it is, not the world as you think it should be, as viewed through eyes colored by your emotions.

In your situation the questions become, 'Where is it written that your husband must not betray you?' or 'Where is it written that he must honor his vows to you, as you have honored your vows to him?' or, and here I will add a few of my own, 'Where is it written that husbands shouldn't lie to their wives about having affairs?' or, and this is a tough one, 'Where is it written that your husband must not commit adultery?' "

Amy: "Well, in the case of the first three, they aren't written anywhere."

BPB: "I disagree. All of these beliefs appear to be written in bold letters in at least one place. Where is that?"

Amy: "You mean in my head?"

BPB: "Exactly. Just because they are written in your head, does that make them true?"

Amy: "I guess not. But what about the fourth question? It *is* written in the Bible that husbands shouldn't commit adultery."

BPB: "You're right, it is written in the Bible 'Thou shalt not commit adultery.' It is one of God's Ten Commandments. Let's see how we can make sense of this. When you were driving to the seminar today, what was the speed limit on the highway?"

Amy: "It's 65 miles per hour."

BPB: "So it is written on the side of the road that the speed limit is 65. May we assume then that everyone on the highway was going 65 miles per hour or less?"

Amy: "I wish! I was going 65 and people were passing me left and right."

BPB: "But how can that be? You just said that it was written on the highway that the speed limit is 65. If it's written there, why isn't everyone going 65 or less? Do you get my point?"

Amy: "Yes, unfortunately I do get it. Just because something is written somewhere, even in the Bible, doesn't necessarily make it true in this world."

BPB: "Now you see the problem with your belief. While it may be written in the Bible that your husband should not commit adultery, God also gave us free will, which allows us to behave contrary to His Commandments. As we speak today, people all over the world are breaking God's Commandments. I do like to remind folks, however, that even though we are free to do whatever we want, we are not free to avoid the consequences of doing whatever we want. Does that make sense?"

Amy: "Absolutely. My husband is free to commit adultery if he wants, but he is not free to avoid the consequences which include shattering his relationship with me and destroying whatever trust the kids had in him as a father."

BPB: "Getting back to your earlier question, 'Shouldn't people keep their promises to each other?' my answer is that the world would definitely be a better place if people kept their promises to each other. But must they keep those promises, sadly the answer is 'no.' "

Amy: "I understand what you are saying."

BPB: "Another question you could ask yourself is, 'Do these beliefs about my husband's behavior help me or hurt me?' "

Amy: "Thinking this way hurts me. It makes me angry, causes me to behave like a jerk in the restaurant, and sends my heart rate through the roof."

BPB: "Right. How about this question, 'Do these beliefs help my important relationships, in this case with my husband and children, or do they hurt those relationships?' "

Amy: "Thinking this way hurts my relationship with my soon-to-be ex-husband. We have three young daughters that we still need to be parents to and my anger gets in the way of us doing what is right for them. Also, the kids see me being angry toward their father all the time and that's not good for them."

BPB: "Do your beliefs solve the problem of your husband having an affair?"

Amy: "No, that is over with now. He made his choice, and now it's up to the rest of us to decide how we want to respond."

BPB: "The last question you could ask is, 'Would your best friend view the activator the same way you do?' "

Amy: "You know, it's interesting that you ask that. Nan is my best friend in the world and for years she has been telling me that my husband was capable of cheating on me. She's been telling me to make a life on my own with the kids before he left us. I guess she was right all along."

Once you courageously complete the process of questioning your beliefs, you are ready to replace your anger-producing beliefs with beliefs that allow you to finally let go of your anger. Those beliefs will make up your effective personal philosophy.

E = <u>Effective Personal Philosophy:</u> There are four important points to remember about the beliefs that make up your effective personal philosophy:

- Beliefs that make up your effective personal philosophy are *preferential* in nature. That is, they are beliefs of preferring, wishing, hoping, desiring and wanting.

- Preferential beliefs are adaptable, flexible and non-dogmatic.

- Preferential beliefs require acceptance of the fact that you have 0% control over the activator.

- Preferential beliefs are ultimately true in the real world.

In this case, Amy's effective belief would take this form:

Amy: "When I married my husband, I made a commitment to him to remain by his side till death do us part. I have lived up to that commitment, and I would have preferred that he do the same. Ultimately, though, I have no control over what he decides to do."

Not surprisingly, once the preferential belief is substituted for the anger-producing belief, the emotional, behavioral and physical consequences noted earlier change.

BPB: "Amy, let's imagine that when you learned of your husband's affair, instead of saying to yourself, 'He must honor his commitment to me!' you thought, 'When I married my husband, I made a commitment to him to remain by his side till death do us part. I have lived up that commitment, and I would have preferred that he do the same. Ultimately, though, I have no control over what he decides to do.' Based on that new belief, what would happen to your anger that started out at around 9 or 10? Would it go up, stay the same, or go down?"

Amy: "It would go down to about a 2 or 3 on that scale. I still wouldn't be happy, but I wouldn't be angry, either. I would be irritated to use your term."

BPB: "Why do I want you to go from being angry in this situation to being irritated?"

Amy: "Because if I am irritated and not angry, chances are I wouldn't behave as badly as I did at the restaurant, my body wouldn't get all messed up, and I would probably be better at solving the problems we are likely to have surrounding our divorce and how to best take care of the kids."

BPB: "That's right, Amy. Now you understand!"

I want to make three final points concerning this dialogue. First, some people mistakenly think that the process Amy and I have just gone through represents an attempt on my part to get her to condone her husband's actions. Nothing could be further from the truth. Personally, I find her husband's decision to have an affair to be reprehensible, and by no means am I trying to get her to view it as "okay." The goal of this exercise is to help Amy let go of her anger toward her husband so she can position herself to handle problems surrounding the dissolution of their marriage in a manner that is most favorable for herself and her children.

Second, I stated earlier in the book that the process of letting go of anger is really a search for the truth. Initially, that may have sounded strange. Here, however, is where we finish the search for the truth by asking the following question:

BPB: "Amy, we are almost at the end of our conversation, but I have just a couple more questions to ask. Which of these two beliefs is true? That your husband *must* not commit adultery, or that you *wish* he hadn't, but you have *no control* over what he does?"

Amy: "The second belief is true."

BPB: "Isn't it interesting how, when you tell yourself lies, you get angry and all worked up, and when you tell yourself what is true the anger goes away?"

Amy: "You're right. I guess I've been telling myself lies for a long time."

> *Once you assemble a personal philosophy composed of beliefs that are true, anger is no longer a problem.*

Third, as you learned in Chapter Two, anger can sometimes be a "secondary emotion" that serves as a mask for other feelings such as hurt, sadness or disappointment. As I work with Amy, I suspect that her anger is a cover for one or more of these other feelings. At times people will spontaneously offer, "You know, I'm really not so angry with my husband as I am profoundly hurt and disappointed over what he has done." Other times, however, probing for that possibility may need to be done. Such was the case with Amy.

BPB: "Amy, you have done a remarkable job and I want to thank you for your help. I am grateful for this chance to talk with you. Before we finish up, one thing comes to my mind and I wanted to run it by you. When I put myself in your position, and imagine that my wife Valerie, to whom I have dedicated my life, has done to me what your husband did to you, I am overcome not with anger, but with waves of hurt and sadness. I wonder if that's not really what's going on with you?"

The anger is now gone. Her eyes are glistening with tears as she slowly nods her head in agreement. I look at her and say, "Amy, take heart. With the passage of time the hurt and sadness will lessen and you and your children make new lives. Hurt and sadness won't kill you. Anger will. What a wonderful gift you have given yourself today: The gift of letting go of your anger."

FINAL THOUGHTS ON LETTING GO OF ANGER

My conversation with Amy ended when she acknowledged that hurt, sadness and disappointment were her real emotional responses to her husband's decision to have an affair. I believe that there is considerable personal power associated with being able to operate from a position of hurt, sadness and disappointment. Let me explain what I mean.

For two years I worked with an organization that sponsored my seminars throughout the country. Though the relationship had been mutually beneficial in the beginning, it became less so with the passage of time. Finally, with the announcement of the upcoming seminar "season," it became clear that they no longer wished to sponsor the topic I most enjoyed presenting on—anger.

My initial response was to anger myself about what I considered to be their poor handling of the matter. I recall wanting to send the president of the organization a rather nasty e-mail, full of finger pointing, accusations and blame, tendering my resignation. If that message had been sent, it would have ended our relationship on a most unpleasant note.

Recall, now, that emotions drive your behaviors. In this case, my anger was driving me to send that e-mail. Rather quickly, however, it dawned on me that I wasn't really angry at their decision; instead, I was deeply saddened and disappointed. Once I understood how I

73

really felt, the contents of my e-mail changed dramatically. Instead of finger pointing, accusations and blame, I sent thanks and expressions of gratitude for the many opportunities they had afforded me over the years. While I still tendered my resignation, I did so in a manner that earned me praise from members of the organization and a legitimate invitation to return should things change in the future.

Understanding your real emotional experience, and then acting based on that experience, dramatically enhances your personal power and effectiveness.

People often ask how long it takes to learn how to let go of anger. There is no specified length of time. In my case, I view the *process* of learning how to let go of my personal anger as a lifelong endeavor. With each passing year the anger- producing beliefs that make up my demanding and commanding personal philosophy lose some of their power, and I move closer to living according to what is true in the world.

I have worked with some people who made the transition from anger to irritation so quickly that it is almost impossible to believe. And, of course, I have worked with some who are simply unwilling to give up on their anger—no matter what the consequences. At the outset I suggested that learning how to relinquish your anger is a journey; my task is to get you started and to supply the tools so you can finish on your own, in your own time.

Be patient with yourself, and expect setbacks, but never stop trying. If you use the approach we have just covered, you will never get angry again, right? Wrong. Chances are excellent that you will accept future invitations from life circumstances to anger yourself. But you will accept fewer invitations and, of those you do accept, you will anger yourself less intensely and for shorter periods of time. It has taken you years to perfect your anger script. Letting go of anger requires constant self-awareness and practice doing that most unnatural of acts—questioning the validity of your own beliefs.

What were once automatic thoughts producing anger will become, instead, automatic thoughts producing irritation. Where once you engaged in self-defeating behaviors growing out of your anger, you now find yourself equipped to solve the problems life throws your way. You have now been given what I consider to be the most powerful psychological tool available for letting go of anger. Whether or not you have the courage to use this tool is completely up to you.

*At times clients suggest that I am teaching them how **NOT** to feel. Nothing could be further from the truth. I want my clients to experience emotions with great intensity—but only those emotions that enhance their lives. Anger is not one of those feelings.*

CHAPTER FOUR

THE MANY FACES OF ANGER

There are four types of temperament:

> *He who is easily angered and easily appeased, his loss is cancelled by his gain.*

> *He whom it is hard to anger and hard to appease, his gain is cancelled by his loss.*

> *He whom it is hard to anger and easy to appease, this is a saintly temperament.*

> *He whom it is easy to anger and hard to appease, this is a wicked temperament.*

The Book of Jewish Values:
A Day to Day Guide to Ethical Living.
Rabbi Joseph Telushkin

As you read the four temperaments, which one are you? Many people who experience real problems with anger are "easy to anger and hard to appease." As the quotation rightly points out, such a temperament is "wicked." This book is about challenging you to develop a more "saintly" temperament, one where you are hard to anger and easy to appease. As you learned in the previous chapter, changing your demanding and commanding personal philosophy to a preferential personal philosophy will assist you in moving toward a more saintly temperament.

Just as there are different temperaments, so, too, are there many different expressions of anger. The more I ponder this topic, coupled with what I learn from the people I counsel as well as those who attend my seminars, the more amazed I am by the various "faces" anger can assume.

ANGER AND CONTROL

WOW BOX

Happiness and freedom begin with a clear understanding of one principle: Some things are within our control, and some things are not. It is only after you have faced up to this fundamental rule… that inner tranquility and outer effectiveness become possible. Epictetus

Just as it appears natural for human beings to experience anger, so is it natural for us to believe that we can control all manner of things external to ourselves. After all, don't we live in a world where science has harnessed the atom and will soon reveal the secrets of the human genetic code? All around us we build dams to control the flow of rivers and prisons to control the flow of "undesirables." We install metal detectors in schools to control students who may behave violently, and we install *mental detectors* to reassure ourselves that the world is a safe, predictable place and that everything is "under control." But is it really?

In our efforts to control the external world, almost always, like children, our reach vastly exceeds our grasp. By definition, anger is the emotion you experience when you are starkly confronted by the realization that your efforts at controlling life circumstances or others have failed. When you attempt to control life circumstances, and they don't unfold the way you believe they should, you make yourself angry. When you attempt to control others, and they don't behave the way you think they should, you anger yourself again. Life is constantly giving you opportunities to learn the limits of what you can and cannot control—yet often you resist learning those lessons. When you fail to learn these lessons, you continue angering yourself.

Letting go of anger requires acceptance of a simple truth:
Outside of your own thoughts, feelings and behaviors,
you control nothing.

As you learned earlier, anger can be difficult to let go of because you may believe that it gets you what you demand. As you get angrier, and people give in to your demands, you conclude that it was your anger that *made* the other person do your bidding; that you could control that person via your anger. There are at least three problems with this assumption:

By believing that your anger helps you control others, you overlook the fact that others have freedom of choice, and that their compliance with your demands is not because your anger made them do anything but, rather, it represents a decision to comply on their part. Second, simply because someone chooses to give in to your angry demands today does not mean that person will do so in the future. Your son may give in to your demand that he complete his homework while plotting how he will repay your attempts at controlling him. When individuals perceive that they have less power than the individual making demands, they may comply outwardly, while seething inside as they wait for an opportunity to even the score.

Children understand keenly that they are not as powerful as adults and often go underground with their anger. I recall adolescent telling me how his father had been trying to control his behavior both at home and at school. One day his father told him to mail an important tax-related document that needed to be postmarked by a certain date.

The young man agreed to mail the letter then "accidentally on pur-
pose" forgot, resulting in his father incurring a sizable tax penalty.
The moral of the story is that when you try to control others, you
eventually learn that "what goes around, comes around."

Third, when others perceive that you are trying to control them, they often do the exact opposite of what you are demanding. The relationship between control, and resistance to control, is made vivid for me by recalling the spaceship *Enterprise* from the *Star Trek* television series. The ship possessed a number of "rays" and "beams" designed to protect it from attack. One such beam was called the "tractor beam." This beam was designed to lock on to an object in space and pull it toward the ship. That is, the beam was designed to control that object.

Even if you've never seen an episode of *Star Trek,* I bet you can guess what the object tries to do once the tractor beam is locked on. Exactly! It does everything in its power to resist that beam and break free. Your anger is like that beam. When another person senses that you are trying to assert control, by locking on with your "anger beam," that person is likely to resist your efforts and try furiously to move away from you. Learning to let go of your anger is about learning how to turn that beam off. Once the beam gets turned off, then something interesting often happens: The object moves towards you—which is, at least in theory, what you wanted all the time. Imagine what would happen to the quality of your relationships if, having changed your personal philosophy, you were able to turn your anger beam off. I think they would improve dramatically.

The next time you are at the beach, bend over and grab a handful
of sand. As you squeeze the sand more tightly, what happens? It
gradually seeps between your fingers. As you try controlling another
person with your anger, what happens to that relationship? It, too,
pours through your fingers and is lost.

Ultimately the belief that you can control another human being is a myth—albeit a myth shared by many. By definition, a myth is "a fiction or half-truth that forms part of an ideology." In this case, it forms part of a faulty personal philosophy. The truth is that, beyond your own thoughts, feelings and behaviors, *you can control no one* or *no-thing.* In a culture that advocates controlling everyone and everything, this can be a bitter pill to swallow. But from my perspective, acknowledging that I cannot control anyone or anything outside of myself has been one of the most psychologically liberating experiences imaginable.

The relationship between anger and control is illustrated nicely via this transcript of an actual radio conversation between a U.S. Navy ship and Canadian authorities off the coast of Newfoundland in October 1995. Not only does trying to control others not work, but you can also appear rather foolish in the process!

Americans: Please divert your course 15 degrees to the north to avoid a collision.

Canadians: Recommend you divert YOUR course 15 degrees to the south to avoid a collision.

Americans: This is the captain of a U.S. Navy ship. I say again, divert YOUR course.

Canadians: No. I say again, you divert YOUR course.

Americans: This is the aircraft carrier *U.S.S. Lincoln*, the second largest ship in the United States fleet. Three destroyers, three cruisers, and numerous support vessels accompany us. I **demand** that you change your course 15 degrees north. That's one five degrees north, or counter mea-

sures will be taken to ensure the safety of this
ship.

Canadians: We are a lighthouse. Your call.

ANGER IN RESPONSE TO CHANGE

> *When considering the future, remember that all situations unfold as
> they do regardless of how we feel about them. Our hopes and fears
> sway us, not the events themselves. Events themselves are imperson-
> al...but to seek out the opportunity in situations requires a great deal
> of courage, for most people around you will persist in interpreting
> events in the grossest terms: success or failure, good or bad, right or
> wrong...What is a "good" event? What is a "bad" event? There is
> no such thing! Epictetus*

WOW BOX

This is one of my favorite quotations from Epictetus. I invite you
to re-read it, at least once, and then to stop for a moment and reflect
on its implications for your life. What makes it even more relevant
is that we live in a world where change, both personal and professional, is coming at an ever-accelerating rate. One of my greatest joys
is working with businesses to help their employees deal more effectively with emotions, such as anger, which can interfere with the
change process. It is for that reason that I have chosen to use a work-
related example for this section. Needless to say the challenges we
experience in response to change are largely the same whether the
change is personal or professional in nature.

At a seminar in the Washington, D.C., area a charming woman
approached me and introduced herself. "Hello, Dr. Barris. My name
is Claire, and this is my husband, Chris. I attended your workshop

last week and really liked it. I brought my husband with me today because I thought he might also need to hear what you have to say." During lunch, Claire, Chris and I discussed his work as the owner of a business-consulting firm. He described how much of his work involved helping employees adjust to the rapid pace of workplace change.

As if conveying an unarguable, eternal truth, Chris went on to note that, "People just don't like change. They view change as a bad thing." I looked at him for a moment, smiled, and suggested, "You know, of course, that change is neither good nor bad. Actually, it's really quite meaningless!" A look of bewilderment spread across his face. "What do you mean change is meaningless?"

BPB: "I can see I caught you off guard with that last statement about change being meaningless. Would you like to understand where I'm coming from when I make that statement?"

Chris: "Absolutely!"

BPB: "One of my favorite teachers was the Greek philosopher Epictetus. Even though he wrote more than 2,000 years ago, he has much of value to say on the topic of change. One of his teachings begins, 'When considering the future, remember that all situations unfold as they do regardless of how we feel about them. Our hopes and fears sway us, not the events themselves.' What do you think he's getting at here?"

Chris: "It sounds like he is saying that we don't control whether or not change takes place in our lives, and that how we feel about change doesn't alter that process. "

BPB: "That's exactly what he is saying. How does the notion of not having any control over the unfolding of events in your professional life strike you?"

Chris: "My initial response is that I don't like it. I'd like to believe that I could control my professional destiny by paying my dues, working harder, learning more, etc."

BPB: "So paying your dues, working harder, and learning more prevented you from leaving your last employer?"

Chris: "I see your point. Despite all those things I still left because I just wasn't happy with the direction my career was taking. I tried telling my boss that all the traveling they expected was really getting to me and it wasn't good for our family since my wife was pregnant with our fourth child."

BPB: "It sounds to me like you were trying to *influence* the circumstances surrounding your previous employment but that ultimately you had no control over what the company expected from you in terms of travel."

Chris: "I guess you're right."

BPB: "How did you feel when you first learned that they wouldn't budge on the travel requirement?"

Chris: "I was pretty angry."

BPB: "Did your anger change the reality of your situation?"

Chris: "No, it didn't change the company's decision in the slightest. I see what Epictetus was getting at about our emotions not changing things."

BPB: "Epictetus also points out that, 'Events themselves are impersonal… but to seek out the opportunity in situations requires a great deal of courage.' What does he mean here?"

Chris: "That from change comes opportunities for those who can find them. He's right about that. After I left the company I took what my wife and I had saved and opened my own consulting business—a decision I've never regretted. That was almost 11 years ago."

BPB: "At the outset of our conversation I suggested that change was essentially meaningless and you were confused. Does it make more sense now?"

Chris: "Now it makes perfect sense. You're right. Change is neither good nor bad—it is meaningless. It's what we decide to do with it that gives change its meaning."

BPB: "Now, Chris, you understand what Epictetus knew 2,000 years ago, which is, 'What is a 'good' event? What is a 'bad' event? There is no such thing!'"

I would like to emphasize a few points growing out of this conversation. You are learning that one characteristic of an activator (such as a change in your employment status) is that it is always meaningless—activators, in and of themselves, carry no meaning. The meaning is not inherent in the activator; rather, the meaning is determined by your *interpretation* of the activator. You give events in your life their meaning—and the meanings you give are based on choices you make. If you give them untrue meanings, you anger yourself. If the meanings you give activators are true, you let go of your anger. Change is a significant activator for most people. The important thing to remember about change is that it is neither "good" nor "bad." It is meaningless or, at the very least, neutral. It is your interpretation of change that determines its "goodness" or "badness."

You will have no control over change occuring either at work or at home. You will only control your response to change.

We noted earlier that the rate of change is increasing. At home and at work, what you think you know today is swept away tomorrow. Although people are bombarded with advice to expect and embrace change, most respond to change with anger, anxiety or a combination of the two. As you learned earlier, not all emotions are helpful. Anger in response to change can have devastating consequences for you.

Personally, anger hinders your interactions with important sources of support like family, friends and co-workers. As you anger yourself over the change process, you are more likely to "circle your wagons," thereby missing out on information that might help you benefit from the change process. Your anger also pushes away the people who are most interested in your well-being. The net effect of your anger is increasing isolation, at precisely the moment when you most need to elicit the support and assistance of others.

Professionally, anger spills over to the company's "bottom line" in a multitude of ways. When you are angry about changes taking place at work, chances are good that you are spending more time at the water cooler expressing your anger to your co-workers than actually doing your job. Anger often makes its way into your interactions with important users of your company's products. Don't fool yourself: All business is built on relationships, and relationships tend to be brittle. All it takes is one angry word from you and a valued customer will begin looking elsewhere to replace your product or service. Anger also interferes with important organizational relationships. Angry supervisors destroy morale, while angry supervisees undermine organizational efforts. Lastly, anger clouds your judgment and ability to solve the problems associated with change. Remember, it is your philosophy toward change that determines the outcome of the process.

VICTIMHOOD

People who regard themselves as victims do not see themselves as in control of their own lives. Whatever happens in their lives happens **to** *them, not* **by** *them.* — Dennis Prager

Just as we have become a culture that worships at the altar of our emotions, so have we become a culture that prizes the status of "victim." The surest way to find an audience in our society involves adopting the victim mantle and then standing back as the world beats a path to your door. An entire industry supports persons wishing to assume victim status. Some in my own profession of psychology have joined this industry—and why not? Victims need therapy and isn't that how we earn our daily crust of bread?

Within the context of this book, the A $\overrightarrow{\text{causes}}$ C Connection we identified earlier is what I refer to as the "victimhood formula." As long as you believe that circumstances cause your anger, you are a victim of whatever life throws your way. The author Dennis Prager accurately notes that victims view life as something that happens **to** them, not **by** them. Rather than being active in the creation of your life, you view yourself as a passive recipient of what life dishes out.

Living according to a philosophy whereby other people or circumstances make you angry means that you have chosen to live as a victim. This is the "anti-victim" book. It's about you accepting responsibility for your own thoughts, feelings and actions—no matter what life throws your way. Aspiring victims need not apply!

I once had the distinct pleasure and privilege to speak before a group of Native American mental health professionals in Oregon. As one of the few non-natives attending, I had an opportunity to learn more about their history and culture via a private exchange with three of the sponsoring tribal elders. Our exchanges, which were very open and honest, included one where a participant, obviously angry, said, "Well, how do you think it is for us? Because of what your people have done, we are now living through the fifth generation of children with Fetal Alcohol Syndrome!" I reminded the speaker that, while European Americans may have contributed to the problem at the outset, many generations had passed since that time. I suggested that the Native American community look at itself, rather than blame others, in order to find a way to deal with this devastating problem.

What About Repressed Anger?

A woman approached me after a seminar and, within 10 minutes, described the entire course of the therapy she had recently undertaken. She reported that her work in therapy had helped her to "finally get in touch with my anger." Needless to say, her well-meaning therapist had encouraged this getting-in-touch process. The therapist believed this process to be important because she had "repressed" her anger for many years. Her question for me was whether I thought she should let her repressed anger "out" in order to *feel* better.

I am still not sure what her therapist meant by "letting it out." Did that mean hitting a pillow? Did it mean aggressively confronting the person who had triggered her anger? Did the therapist mean that she should scream at the top of her lungs? You know that these approaches offer no long-term solution to the problem of her anger. You also know that her life circumstances did not make her angry; rather, it was how she chose to view those circumstances that caused her anger.

Getting in touch with repressed anger and then finding a suitable way to let it out is not the answer. Letting anger out causes problems that last far longer than any momentary relief. If this woman could let go of her anger, as you are learning how to do, then letting it out or keeping it in really wouldn't matter, would it?

ANGER AS A DEFENSE

A beautiful, highly successful woman entered therapy stating that her husband was threatening to leave her unless she got help for her frequent angry outbursts. Although I do not find it particularly helpful or efficient to spend much time discussing my clients' pasts, there are times when such an exploration helps me better understand the origins of the beliefs that make up their faulty personal philosophy.

This client discussed her father, an angry man steeped in the command-and-control mentality of the military. Although she adored him, and considered their relationship to be good, she feared his disapproval and would do almost anything to avoid it. For her, disapproval carried the specter of being "cut off" or abandoned by her father, a notion that was the source of much discomfort and anxiety for her.

At the outset of each new dating relationship, everything went well. Eventually, however, she noticed her normally pleasant demeanor becoming increasingly more shrill and angry. This situation escalated until her male companion, no longer willing to tolerate her outbursts, left her.

Recall that anger pushes people away from you. No one enjoys being in your company when you are angry. Unable to tolerate the notion that her boyfriend might leave, the client used her anger as a means of pushing him away from her first. In this respect her anger served as part of a self-fulfilling prophecy in which what she most feared, abandonment, is exactly what her anger created. Her anger served as a "preemptive strike" against her partner.

In cases like this, the task for the client is to understand that anger is serving as a mask for feelings of anxiety surrounding possible abandonment. Letting go of her anger would not only improve her marriage, but also make it easier for her to rewrite the mental script that is producing her anxiety.

NARCISSISM, ANGER AND THE AGE OF ENTITLEMENT:
WHY THE WORLD IS AN ANGIER PLACE IN WHICH TO LIVE

According to Greek mythology, Echo was a nymph who fell in love with the spectacularly handsome Narcissus. It was Echo's fate that her love for Narcissus would not be returned and, having been spurned, she soon died a wretched death. One day a young woman who had also been rejected by Narcissus asked the gods that the young man come to feel the pain of loving another and not having that love returned. The goddess Nemesis heard the prayer and granted the young woman's request.

In the mountains where Narcissus walked there was a fountain with crystal-clear water. As he stooped to take a drink, there in the water he saw his own image that he mistook for some beautiful water-spirit living in the fountain. He tried to kiss and embrace the water-spirit—only to have it flee his every effort to share his affections with it. He could not break away from his fascination with the image in the water and, after the passage of time, his beauty, youth and vigor declined until he died at the foot of the fountain. The image Narcissus had fallen in love with was his own—he had fallen in love with himself!

A friend noted that one reason why readers enjoyed my first book was that it included stories of my own struggles with anger. I would like to think that the same spirit of openness has guided my work in this book. I can honestly say that this section was at once the easiest, and at the same time most difficult, portion of the book for me to write. It was the easiest because this is the face of anger with which I am personally most familiar. It was the most difficult because, unlike the story above, I didn't always like the face peering back at me from the crystal-clear fountain.

This book considers anger, from a psychological perspective, to be the product of your untrue beliefs, which then create a demanding and commanding personal philosophy. When trying to understand why the world is angrier than it used to be, and why anger will only continue to increase, it is crucial to understand the *philosophical basis* for that anger. The philosophical bases for the increase in anger we see today are related to the intertwined problems of *narcissism* and *entitlement*.

From the tragic story of Narcissus our language acquired the term "narcissistic" to describe persons who have an exaggerated love of, and focus upon, themselves. The personal philosophy of the narcissist has many different facets, of which the following are the most important:

- a grandiose sense of their own self-importance;

- a belief that they are unique and special people who can only be understood and appreciated by other unique and special people;

- a tendency to lack empathy;

- unrealistic expectations of others which, when unmet, lead to outbursts of anger; and,

- a keen sense of entitlement which, when violated, results in outbursts of anger.

Underpinning the narcissistic personal philosophy is a variety of entitlement-related beliefs. To believe that you are entitled to some benefit means believing that you are "due" or "owed" that benefit; oftentimes with you having done nothing to earn it. Narcissistic people believe that they are entitled to all manner of things simply because they decide to show up for life each day! Many people live according to an overwhelming sense of entitlement that includes the following beliefs:

- "I am entitled to be treated fairly at all times."

- "I am entitled to a high-paying job, new car, big screen television, nice house, etc."

- "I am entitled to be cared for by my family, friends, spouse and the government."

- "I am entitled to what I want, when I want it, without expending too much effort or experiencing any discomfort in trying to obtain what life owes me."

- "I am entitled to respect at all times and to never have someone say or do something I may deem offensive."

- "I am entitled to free health care and prescription privileges."

- "I am entitled to buy gas at $1 a gallon and not a penny more."

- "I am not entitled to the pursuit of happiness. I am entitled to happiness itself."

Recasting these entitlement-related beliefs into the anger-producing beliefs that become part of a demanding and commanding personal philosophy is easy:

- "I *should* be treated fairly at all times."

- "I *must* have a high-paying job, a new car, big screen

television, nice house, etc."

- "Others (friends, spouses, family, the government, etc.) *ought to* take care of me."

- "I *shouldn't* have to expend too much effort or experience any discomfort in obtaining what life owes me."

- "No one *should* ever say or do anything to me that I deem offensive."

- "I *ought to* have free health care and prescription privileges."

- "I *shouldn't* have to pay more than a $1 a gallon for gas."

- "I *shouldn't* have to pursue happiness; the world *should* just give it to me."

Entitlement-related beliefs are among the most extreme forms of demanding and commanding beliefs.

The potential list of entitlement-related beliefs is endless and, I'm sorry to say, only getting longer. The problem with your entitlement-related beliefs is that, like all anger-producing beliefs, they are untrue. What is true is that:

Life doesn't care what you believe you are entitled to!

When life denies you what you believe you are entitled to, you are prone to making yourself very angry. When you reflect on the whole notion of entitlement, however, you will immediately be struck by the reality that no one, including yourself, is entitled to anything. The following stories illustrate my point.

One group member comes immediately to mind when I think of entitlement-related anger. Shelly, a former nurse in the Marines, cared for sick and dying children at a local hospital. As a result of her many good works, she believed her own family to be immune from the profound sadness she encountered on a daily basis. She entered an anger management group not long after leukemia was diagnosed in her 10-year-old son. In addition to her anger at the court for ordering her to attend my program (over a disagreement she allegedly had with her husband), she was profoundly angry about her child's illness. It quickly became apparent that her beliefs included, among others: "I've helped all these other children and families throughout the years, so these things shouldn't happen to my family. I should have a life free of pain because of all I've done to help others."

As is my style, I worked on getting her to look at how her beliefs were contributing to her anger, but she was not ready to let go of them. She stormed out of the first session, and I was convinced that she wouldn't return. And she didn't—until three weeks later. At the outset of the group she graciously apologized for her behavior and said, "You know, you were right about why I was so angry that first session. I mean, I know all about that 'bad things happen to good people' stuff; it's just that I couldn't believe that this was happening to *me*. I guess we all think we are special; that we won't have to go through what other people go through. You know, since I figured this all out, I spend a lot less energy being angry, and a lot more time being grateful for those moments my son and I have together."

Another example of entitlement-related anger I've never forgotten centered on the experiences of the figure skater Nancy Kerrigan. You may recall that Nancy was scheduled to compete for a place on the U.S. Olympic Figure Skating Team when an assailant hired by her main competitor, Tonya Harding, tried to shatter her knee. That week's issue of *Newsweek* ran a picture of Kerrigan on the front page, grimacing in pain, under the caption, "Why?" Kerrigan seemed to be asking herself the question, "Why did this happen to me?" which, transformed into a statement, sounds like the anger-producing belief, "This *shouldn't* have happened to me!"

Had Kerrigan been my client, and had she discussed with me her anger surrounding this event, my first question to her would have been, "Nancy, can you give me one reason why this *shouldn't* have happened to you? What makes you so special that you are *entitled* to avoid the bad things that happen to the rest of us?" I've always assumed (during this fictional exchange) that, as she pondered my questions, her anger would lessen as she realized that she was neither so special, nor entitled, to avoid the travails each of us experiences at some point in our lives. As the Bible says, "It rains equally on the just and unjust." And so it does.

As I suggested at the outset of this section, I also struggle with a narcissistic personal philosophy containing a variety of entitlement-related beliefs. I acquired this philosophy from observing my father who, for many years, was considered one of the best criminal trial attorneys in the country. His income allowed me to travel extensively, to attend private schools, to indulge my passion for anything with either two or four wheels, and to generally live life at a material level known to only a privileged few.

Growing up in this world I soon came to believe myself entitled to the "good life"—though, of course, I had done nothing to create that life for myself. Along the way, life tried teaching me lessons regarding my sense of entitlement, but I steadfastly refused to listen. For example, when life once refused my demand for a high-paying job (though I had not finished college—I was too smart to waste my time finishing college!), I angered myself greatly. "How dare the world refuse me what I am entitled to?" "Doesn't the world know who the hell I am?" I howled in protest.

My powerful sense of entitlement might have remained to this day were it not for life giving me one more chance to learn what I really was, and was not, entitled to. The lesson began when the phone in my Seattle apartment rang loudly one morning. Sleepily, I stumbled from the bedroom to the kitchen and picked up the receiver. "Hello," I said faintly. It was my brother calling from New York. "Brad, you need to get home right away. Dad killed himself." I do not recall what I said next. It really doesn't matter. What I do recall, however, was the funeral and the long flight back to Seattle with only my thoughts as company.

During that flight I began to glimpse the notion that my life had been, for the most part, a lie. I had basked in the reflected glory of a successful father and, in the process, had created for myself a personal philosophy built upon the fiction of a whole host of entitlement-related beliefs. At that moment I finally understood what life had been trying to teach me all along—that I was not entitled to anything!

Our society is angrier because we are currently living through what I call the *Age of Entitlement*—a moment in history when everyone believes that he or she is entitled to, or owed, every resource society has to offer. From free housing to a free education; from free medical care to a subsidized income, the march toward declaring almost everything in our culture an "entitlement" is grounded in the material wealth we enjoy, coupled with the political and social changes that have shaped our country during the last 50 years. While no doubt well-intentioned, those who pressed for expanding the notion of what constitutes an entitlement actually created a breeding ground for much of the anger and resentment around us today. Just as a fire needs oxygen to burn, so does anger need incendiary anger-producing beliefs regarding entitlement in order to flourish.

When a teenage burglary suspect was caught and questioned, he stated, "I don't know what the big deal is—they had stuff I wanted so I took it."

In addition to fueling much of the anger we see around us, this pervasive sense of entitlement robs us of one of life's noblest and most uplifting emotional experiences—the ability to feel gratitude. Gratitude is the state of being grateful or thankful for someone or something in your life. Think about it for a moment. When you believe you are entitled to something, and do not get what you believe you are entitled to, how do you feel? Very angry. Conversely, when you believe that you are entitled to something, and do get what you believe you are entitled to, how do you feel? Empty because, after all, you simply got that which was your due. Accepting that you are ultimately not entitled to anything douses the flames of anger and opens a pathway to experiencing gratitude.

If you don't think there is a world of difference between operating out of a stance of gratitude, as opposed to a stance of entitlement, give it a try. The world will like you better and you will like yourself a whole lot better. I am always at my best when I set aside my entitlement-related beliefs and live out of gratitude.

When Worlds Collide: Anger and Fantasy

The relationship between anger and fantasy, while not immediately apparent, is nonetheless compelling. I have long believed that we each live our lives somewhere along a continuum between two conflicting internal worlds—the "World of Should" and the "World of Is."

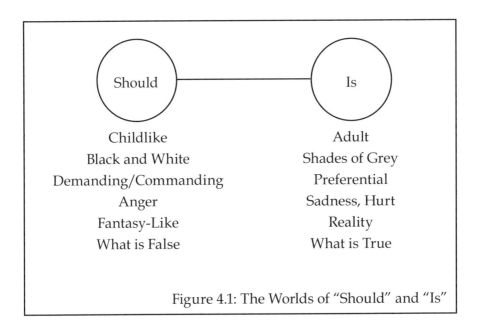

Figure 4.1: The Worlds of "Should" and "Is"

The "World of Should" is a childlike place where everything is neatly defined in black-and-white terms. There is no ambiguity in the World of Should. For the "Should-person," things are either right or wrong. People and their behaviors are either good or bad. There is no middle ground. The World of Should is a place where things should, must and ought to be certain ways; if they aren't, then anger is the appropriate emotional response.

As is the case with children, the notions of fairness and unfairness are very important in the World of Should. Should-people demand that life be fair (at least according to *their* definition of fairness); that they should always get what they want, when they want it, without delay or interference from others. If the Should-person treats others well, then others, such as bosses, children and spouses must respond in kind. Because of their hard work, people living in the World of Should believe that they are entitled to rewards. Should-people demand that the "system" punish "bad people," all the while raining its blessings on "good folks" like themselves. In the World of Should all parents love and support their children, while every child appreciates, loves and obeys his or her parents. On and on it could go!

The World of Should is a perfect world because it's the world exactly the way you think it should, must and ought to be. What a wonderful place the "World of Should" would be—if only it weren't a fantasy existing solely in your mind.

As you would expect, the "World of Is" anchors the opposite end of the continuum from the World of Should. Most people refer to the World of Is as the "real world." "Is-people" live as fully functioning adults. They accept that the world is often ambiguous and uncertain and that successful life is lived in shades of gray. Is-people prefer that they be treated fairly, but understand that life can be both fair and unfair at any moment. They appreciate that the only thing they can control, when confronted by unfairness, is their own response.

Is-people treat others well, but don't demand that others always respond in kind. In the World of Is, hard work is sometimes rewarded and other times not, and in almost all cases you must wait for what you want instead of getting it immediately. In the World of Is, bad things sometimes happen to good people. Lastly, while Is-people prefer, hope, want and wish for certain things to occur in their lives, when their hopes are unrealized they respond with feelings of sadness, hurt and disappointment—but not anger.

When the World of Should and the World of Is collide, as they always will, which one prevails? The World of Is wins every time! Ponder this proposition:

The world is exactly the way it should be.
It doesn't have to be any way, other than the way it is.

As your understanding of the material in this book deepens and strengthens, you will spend less time living in the World of Should, and more time living in the World of Is. Fully functioning adults live in the World of Is. Adults, who think and behave like children, populate The World of Should. A child "pitching a fit" is really no different than an adult angering him or herself. Aren't both really demanding that they get their way? Aren't both really insisting that the world give them what they believe they should, must and ought to have?

<hr>

Anger vs. Passion

<hr>

I have learnt through bitter experience the one supreme lesson: to conserve my anger, and as heat conserved is transmuted into energy, even so our anger controlled can be transmuted into a power that can move the world. —Mohandas K. Gandhi

When discussing the notion of social injustice, many seminar participants question my suggestion that their goal should be to let go of anger. They believe that anger motivates them to redress social injustices. For the following reasons, I must respectfully disagree with their position.

Recall the definition of anger we agreed upon earlier. From a psychological perspective, anger is defined as the emotion humans experience when:

- they live according to an untrue personal philosophy that is demanding and commanding in nature. This philosophy emphasizes what the person believes they should or must get from the world or others.

- their personal philosophy emphasizes what they believe they are entitled to.

- their personal philosophy is starkly confronted by the realization that they cannot control others.

- someone violates one or more of the strongly held beliefs that make up their personal philosophy.

- the sympathetic nervous system is activated.

Accompanying anger is:

- an increased likelihood of aggressive behavior.

- seriously diminished problem-solving skills.

- less-effective parenting skills.

- impaired relationships.

- an orientation towards the past.

- a resistance to change.

- a tendency towards embitterment.

Based upon this definition, angering yourself while pursuing the redress of a particular social injustice would make you *less effective* in trying to achieving your goals. The angrier you became, the more likely you would be to behave aggressively and, in so doing, alienate important sources of support for your cause. Your ability to problem-solve would be impaired, thereby increasing the probability that your attempted solutions would make the problem worse. Finally, since anger orients you to the past, hinders your efforts at change, and tends to embitter you, you will focus on perceived past injustices to the exclusion of present and future opportunities. Since yours is the only "just" position, your views will alienate others at precisely the moment when flexibility would best serve your interests. You will grow to hate your "oppressor" and, in the process, will destroy yourself. I wonder what part of the world this describes?

> *Passion tries not to alienate those who see*
> *things differently, whereas anger does not care.*

Where people err is in equating anger with passion. To seek passionately to right a social injustice is one thing; to use anger is quite another. Passion, itself a powerful emotion, can be controlled, while anger often cannot. Passion, unlike anger, motivates people without blinding them to what needs to be done in order to further their interests.

Was Martin Luther King an angry man? Was Gandhi an angry man? Most people answer "no" to those questions. Yet both men led movements that changed their respective cultures. I suggest that both men were passionate in their pursuit of justice. They knew that, if they got angry, they might say and do things that would give their oppressors the rope with which to hang them. Using carefully controlled passion, rather than unbridled anger, allowed them to change the world.

Anger and Blame

WOW BOX

If it is our thoughts about things that torment us rather than the things themselves, it follows that blaming others is silly. Therefore, when we suffer setbacks, disturbances or grief, let us never place the blame on others, but on our own attitudes. Epictetus

Why do we so easily blame others for our anger? You have learned how to recognize the language of anger and blame. That language is expressed in the A $\overrightarrow{causes}$ C Connection discussed earlier. Statements like, "You made me angry when you didn't take out the trash!" or "You really pissed me off when you forgot to pick up the dry cleaning!" are blaming statments. While blame is everywhere; personal accountability is much harder to find.

WOW BOX

One of the signs of the dawning of moral progress is the gradual extinguishing of blame. We see the futility of finger pointing. The more we examine our attitudes and work on ourselves, the less apt we are to be swept away by stormy emotional reactions in which we seek easy explanations for unbidden events. Epictetus

I suspect the reason why we so easily blame others for our anger is that, for most people, anger is an unpleasant emotional experience. Most people do not enjoy getting angry. People tend to believe that if something is unpleasant, surely they could not be the architects of that unpleasant experience. If something is unpleasant, it must be something others do to us, rather than being something we do to ourselves. We love blaming others for our own distress. As you are learning, it takes courage to acknowledge the role you play in the generation and maintenance of your own anger. Letting go of anger means letting go of blaming others for your anger.

WOW BOX

Small-minded people habitually reproach others for their own misfortunes. Average people reproach themselves. Those who are dedicated to a life of wisdom understand that the impulse to blame something or someone is foolishness, that there is nothing to be gained in blaming, whether it be others or oneself. Epictetus

ANGER AND SHAME

Shame is one of the emotions researchers have identified as common to all humans. Most researchers agree that shame is the result of a strong sense of guilt, embarrassment or disgrace. Like anger, it can be a very powerful emotional experience. Unlike anger, however, appropriate amounts of shame can be beneficial since the goal of shame is to point the individual toward changing behaviors that are contrary to the person's personal philosophy.

Some authors contend that anger is a product of shame. While I find their arguments unpersuasive, there does appear to be an important connection between anger and shame for some people. The connection is found in the fact that shame is an emotion that accompanies being "dis-covered." Shame is what we feel when our inappropriate behavior is uncovered and made available for all to see. It is the emotion we experience when we are laid bare psychologically as the world passes judgment on the choices we make.

As you learned earlier, anger can serve as a mask or cover for more primary emotional experiences—the notion of anger as a secondary emotion. Shame is an example of a primary emotional experience. For some people, however, the prospect of experiencing shame is psychologically overwhelming. They cannot tolerate being dis covered. They cannot bear looking at themselves openly and honestly which, of course, shame requires of us.

Rather than experiencing shame, these individuals transform that emotion into anger. Their anger, always directed toward those who have unmasked them, allows them to feel powerful and potent again, where once their shame had made them feel weak. Their anger allows them to point fingers at, and blame, the people who brought their transgressions to light.

While getting angry has all these supposed advantages, it also postpones the learning process. These individuals focus on accusing and blaming others, while neglecting to evaluate and correct their own behavior. The strategy of converting shame into anger may work in the short term, but seldom does life allow it to work in the long term. At some point, life will teach the shamed person a lesson.

The politician had been "dis-covered." Rather than acknowledging his shame, he wagged his finger, stared defiantly into the television camera, and angrily proclaimed his innocence. "I never had sexual relations with that young woman!" he declared. Shame converted into anger? You decide.

PULLING IT ALL TOGETHER:
SOME FINAL THOUGHTS ON ANGER

It's time to conclude our discussion of the various faces of anger. One question asked repeatedly at my seminars is, "How do you defuse anger in other people?" Given the frequency with which it is asked, this must be a major interpersonal problem.

The technique for defusing anger is actually quite simple. As the other person angrily engages you, it's important to find something in their argument with which you can agree. When someone is angry with me, there is almost always one part of the person's argument—no matter how small—that I can agree with. If I can't find anything to agree with, I can still help defuse the situation by letting the person know that I appreciate how upset they are and that I am trying to understand their position. Once it registers that you are "hearing" their argument, the person will tend to calm down quickly.

*Defusing anger is about taking
your sails out of the other person's wind!*

Both gratitude and humor are powerful antidotes to anger. Humor and anger are products of how you perceive the world. I have learned that many of my anger-producing beliefs are quite funny once exposed to the light of day. In years past I would upset myself greatly while stuck in traffic. Now, in order to let go of my anger, I roll down the windows in my car and begin screaming at the top of my lungs:

"Who do these people think they are? Don't they know who I am? I am the great Dr. Barris! I have people to heal! They should just get the hell out of my way—clear a path and let me go through—and then they can all come together and wait."

Not only am I indulging my narcissism here, but these beliefs are also both humorous and ridiculous in the extreme. Developing an appreciation for the absurd nature of your anger-producing beliefs will lead to more laughter and less anger in your life.

Throughout this book you are learning that anger is almost always a choice. You would never hear me say, "I was driving to work this morning, a guy cut me off, and he really made me angry!" That statement would imply that I had no choice but to get angry. As you have read, however, it is not the activator (cutting me off) that makes me angry, but rather how I choose to think about that activator. Periodically I will remark, "This guy cut me off in traffic and I *chose to* anger myself." By phrasing it that way, I remind myself that I have a choice regarding whether or not to get angry in a given situation.

Ed Nottingham, Ph.D., helps his clients understand the relationship between activators and their anger by having them imagine an activator handing them an "invitation" to upset themselves. Think about it like you would an invitation to a party. Most invitations list the nature of the party, its location and time, and end with "RSVP." The RSVP requests that the recipient respond either by accepting or declining the invitation.

Your response to anger works in much the same way. When the activator does something you think he or she shouldn't have, or doesn't do something you think he or she should have, that activator is sending you an invitation to anger yourself. Since it is your choice whether or not to accept the invitation, I would strongly recommend a polite, "No thanks!"

> *At the conclusion of this section of my seminar, I always give one person in the audience a "pop quiz." I look the lucky person in the eye, extend the middle finger of my left hand and then, once the laughter dies down, ask, "If you've been paying attention to what we've discussed today, you can tell me what this gesture means." If* **you've** *been paying attention, you should be able to come up with the correct answer to this quiz as well. What does the gesture mean? The answer is found on page 173!*

CHAPTER FIVE

THE FIRST STRATEGY: SELF-DISCIPLINE BEFORE OTHER-DISCIPLINE

In self-discipline one makes a "disciple" of oneself. One is one's own teacher, trainer, coach and "disciplinarian." It is an odd sort of relationship, paradoxical in its own way, and many of us do not handle it very well. There is much unhappiness and personal distress in the world because of failures to control tempers, appetites, passions and impulses. "Oh, if only I had stopped myself" is an all too familiar refrain.

The Book of Virtues, *William J. Bennett*

When I speak to parents and teachers, their first request is always for "strategies" they can employ when dealing with children—especially difficult children. By strategies they mean specific things they can either say or do in response to the child's behavior. This reactive stance requires that the parent apply psychological or behavioral techniques to the child to eliminate behaviors deemed "inappropriate," and replace them with "appropriate" ones.

This approach views the child—and the child alone—as the problem. I refer to this as the "unidirectional approach" to dealing with children. With this approach, the parent or teacher drops the child off in a therapist's or school counselor's office and demands that the professional "fix" the child. The caregiver assumes that all will be right with the world after the professional has applied the appropriate techniques to the "fixed" child.

Most professionals working with children understand that few children are, in and of themselves, the sole problem. More often, the problems that children are treated for are the outgrowth of an *interaction* between the child and one or more adults in the child's world. This means that the problem is not unidirectional, but *bi-directional*, in nature.

Assume for the moment that the problem is truly bi-directional, and assume that parents and teachers possess psychological resources significantly more advanced than those of children. Given these assumptions, wouldn't it make sense for parents and teachers to first work on correcting their behaviors that contribute to the child's problems, before attempting to work directly on changing the child's behaviors?

Self-discipline is a term used frequently in our culture, but do we really understand what it means? The root of the word discipline is found in the word "disciple." A disciple is "one who embraces and assists in spreading the teaching of another." To be a disciple means not only to be a kind of follower, but to also be a teacher. Self-discipline, therefore, is a form of self-teaching, or self-instruction, in the art of managing one's self. Parents and teachers would be well served to first *instruct themselves* in self-management (self-discipline) before attempting to instruct their children in self-management (other-discipline). How many parents and teachers do you know who demonstrate self-discipline? Precious few. As a parent or teacher, do *you* operate from a position of self-discipline? Most likely not.

I discuss issues surrounding parenting near the end of my seminar on anger. Invariably, I ask the following question: "How many of you who either have children or work with children can honestly say that you exercise self-discipline—where self-discipline is defined as moving toward mastery of your own thoughts, feelings and behaviors? Please raise your hand." The silence is deafening as no hand is raised.

When adults bring children to me to fix (as if I were some kind of psychological auto mechanic!) because the children are out of control, it is often the case that the adults themselves lack self-discipline and are out of control. I recall a mother and her 12-year-old son. She appeared at her wit's end with the boy, who refused to do his homework, stayed out with his friends beyond their agreed-upon curfew, and was at times physically combative with her. Although she intended to leave her son in my office while she went shopping, I asked her to stay and give me some background information concerning his home life.

"Dr. Barris, I just don't know what to do," she said. "I can't control him anymore. Johnny's father and I divorced when he was about 8. His father still lives in town but doesn't spend any time with Johnny except for a few minutes around Christmas, when he drops off some crummy little gift. Not long after he left us, Johnny's dad started shacking up with his new girlfriend, and pretty soon he had another son by her. The fact is that he's a no-good S.O.B. who doesn't give a damn about Johnny! I've tried finding Johnny a new daddy but once they meet him they don't want to have anything to do with raising some other guy's kid. And in some ways I can understand why, because Johnny and his Daddy are like two peas in a pod. Most of the time they're both good for nothing." Off to the side—as if he weren't there—listens Johnny, shoulders slumped, his face buried in his chest.

Another mother recounted the following story about her 5-year-old son. Apparently he was watching television one morning and saw an ad for a new cereal. Later that day they went grocery shopping. The boy saw the cereal on the shelf and demanded that his mother purchase it for him. The cereal was rather expensive and she replied that they couldn't afford it. The child threw himself on the ground and began pitching a fit. "What did you do then?" I asked. "The only thing I could do, I bought him the box of cereal," she replied. "I couldn't let all the other mothers think that I couldn't control my child!"

> *You don't have to be the "Bride of B.F. Skinner" to understand*
> *that rewarding bad behavior results in more bad behavior!*

Is it any wonder that these children are unruly? Is it any wonder that these children are out of control? One thing people most value most about my books is the consistent focus on how we are often the source of our problems. So it is with parenting and teaching children. When you are having difficulty with children—especially very young children—the first place you need to look for answers is in the mirror. Rather than focusing your energy on trying to change or control them, look at how you can change yourself. If you cannot manage yourself, how in the world can you teach your children to manage themselves?

> *I liken the mind of a child to the soil of the most fertile garden the world has ever known. As children watch how the adults around them handle life's problems, it is akin to the adults spreading seeds upon that soil. Because the soil is so rich, every seed germinates and takes root.*
>
> *Just as every seed does not result in the development of a plant that is helpful to the garden, neither does every emotion and behavior displayed by adults result in children developing healthy emotions and behaviors of their own. Much of what this book describes involves weeding your "psychological garden" by identifying anger-produc-*

ing beliefs and then pulling them out at the root. By practicing self-discipline parents reduce the amount of "weeding" their children need to do later in life.

Throughout this book you have been learning how to let go of your anger no matter what challenges life throws your way. Letting go of anger means that you are moving toward mastering your own thoughts, feelings and behaviors. Self-mastery is the essence of self-discipline. Most children witness your self-mastery, respect it and will seek to emulate you. Only after disciplining yourself do you possess the kind of *authentic* strength that positions you to effectively discipline children.

Expecting children to exercise self-discipline, when you are unable to do so yourself, is really, "Do as I say, not as I do." That approach didn't work when you were a child. It still doesn't work today!

DISTINGUISHING DISCIPLINE FROM PUNISHMENT

Disciplining children is not the same as punishing them. By definition, disciplining children is about teaching them important life lessons. Punishment, by definition, is about getting children to alter their behavior by inflicting pain on them. As you learned earlier, a relationship exists between anger and punishment, and between irritation and discipline.

Think about your own experience. Isn't it the case that when you are angry, and demanding that your child alter his or her behavior, that you are much more likely to reach into your parenting toolbox and pull punishment out as the approach you use? When angry, aren't you much more likely to behave aggressively toward everyone, including your children? Once you let go of your anger, you position yourself to use discipline as the primary means of *influencing* children so they will choose to alter their own behavior.

Why do so many parents and teachers initially choose punishment instead of discipline? There are a number of reasons. First, you will recall that anger has become the automatic or default emotional response for many people when dealing with problems, including problems with children. With anger as the default emotional response, it only makes sense that a more aggressive, punitive stance toward children will follow. Punishment is a behavioral response consistent with the emotion anger.

Second, parents and teachers often make the erroneous connection that it was their punishment of the child that made him or her stop a particular objectionable behavior. This misperception reinforces their use of punishment because they believe that punishment worked. What has really occurred, however, is something quite different. Punishment didn't make the child do anything; rather, the child decided at some point that he or she no longer wished to experience further punishment and ceased the particular behavior.

A third problem with punishment is that children often decide not to engage in certain behaviors, for which they have been punished in the past, but only as long as the threat of punishment is immediately present. Once the threat of immediate punishment is lifted, children frequently resume their objectionable behaviors. This explains why Johnny is such an "angel" at home, where punishment is immediate and sure, while being a "holy terror" everywhere else. Johnny's behavior conforms to acceptable standards when the threat of immediate punishment is present, which means that he has failed to acquire one of the most basic life skills—the internalized regulation of his own behavior.

Fourth, punishment, and the anger that drives it, is based on the myth that parents and teachers can control children. By now you know that you have 0% control over the activators in your life— including children. When parents and teachers attempt to control children a variety of responses can be predicted. The child will either furiously resist your efforts at control and act out; or he or she will comply outwardly, while planning how to "settle the score" at a later date. Efforts at controlling children set the stage for passive-aggressive behaviors where anger is expressed in less direct, often more devious, ways.

The myth that parents and teachers can control children fails to recognize that children are free to make choices concerning whether or not to continue certain behaviors. Punishment may appear to work for some children, but only if the child decides that he or she no longer wishes to experience further punishment. Ultimately, the decision to either continue or discontinue certain behaviors resides exclusively with the child. In other words, you can't make a child do anything.

> *"When my 21-year-old was only 5 he taught me that I couldn't make him do anything. Once I realized that, my life as a parent became a lot more fun." Seminar participant, Santa Fe, NM.*

When I suggest to parents and teachers that they cannot control children a minority will knowingly smile and agree; while the vast majority will become perplexed, then agitated, fearful and angry. One seminar participant in Fairbanks, Alaska, went so far as to describe me as being "full of crap!" when I suggested that she had no control over her children.

Adults become perplexed because no one has ever suggested such a thing to them before and because they always believed that their parents controlled them via punishment. Once the confusion lifts, parents and teachers often become agitated, fearful and angry because, after listening to me explain why it is not possible to control children, they realize that what I am saying is true—and that I have taken from them the only tool they felt competent to use when dealing with children.

If you still don't believe that punishment doesn't make a child's behavior change, then I give to you—as living, breathing proof—what I refer to as *punishment-resistant* children. The frequency with which parents, teachers and mental health providers now see these types of children and adolescents is frightening. Despite losing every possible privilege and experiencing every form of physical punishment short of child abuse, these children still refuse to alter their behaviors. Having been punished all of their lives, they no longer respond to any type of punishment. They have become punishment resistant.

In the case of a punishment-resistant child, the adult's need to control is usually so great that each time the child refuses to change their behavior, the adult angers himself or herself and ups the ante by threatening to increase the punishment. At this point all parties are locked in a gigantic tug-of-war.

The tug-of-war dialogue between a father and his 15 year-old son might sound like this:

Father (picking up his end of the rope): "Son, I understand that you have a math exam on Friday. I guess you'll be staying home tonight to start studying, right?"

Son (picking up his end of the rope): "Well, Dad, in a world where parents don't care about the academic achievement of their children, I am flattered by your interest. But actually I'm not staying home tonight and I'm not studying for my math exam."

Father (tugging back): "Son, I really don't care whether or not you are flattered by my interest. You're going to park your butt in that chair and start studying, mister!"

Son (tugging back): "I can see you are up to your old tricks again, Dad. All I can tell you is this: I will be studying tonight, but it won't be math and it won't be here. I'm planning on studying human anatomy over at Sue Ellen's tonight! See ya!"

Who wins this tug-of-war every time? While you can argue that there are no winners in this exchange, the fact remains that the child wins every time because he or she has more time and energy than you do. Why would a parent or teacher get locked into a tug-of-war with a child, knowing that they were destined to lose? It makes no sense. The only way out of this struggle is for the parent or teacher to drop his or her end of the rope.

Parents and teachers drop their end of the rope by reminding themselves that, while they would *prefer* children behave in certain ways, ultimately they cannot control their children. Once the parent or teacher drops his or her end of the rope, the above dialogue changes dramatically:

Father: "You know son, you and I have been going round and round with this math studying deal for months now, and it's not getting us anywhere, so I've decided to stop playing this game. But before I do, I want to make sure you understand a few things.

First, if you don't study for your math test Friday, chances are pretty good that you will fail. If you fail enough exams, you will likely fail math for the year. If you fail math for the year, you'll be taking it over again in the summer. Are we clear?"

Son: "Sure, Dad!"

Six months later, one of two things will have happened. In a perfect world, Johnny will have gotten the message, studied and passed math for the year. In an imperfect world, Johnny will not have studied and fail. Assuming the latter, he comes in from school on his final day, sticks his report card under your nose, and begins screaming, "What a crummy Dad you are! You let me fail math and now I have to take it during summer school! None of the other parents let their kids fail math!"

Given this scenario, the your response is ready-made, "Johnny, you remember the conversation we had six months ago concerning the consequences of your not studying math? It sounds to me like you're pretty angry about having to go to summer school. If you are angry with anyone, I think you need to be angry with yourself. End of discussion."

Parents and teachers who drop their end of the rope accept that children are free to make whatever choices they want, but they also inform children that they are NOT free to avoid the potentially negative consequences of those choices. This is the notion of natural consequences—those consequences that flow naturally from the choices, both good and bad, that children make. If handled properly, natural consequences can teach children life's most important lessons.

As a parent or teacher, your task is to guide children by establishing a range of choices in any given situation, and then allowing them to choose from within that range. The range of choices becomes greater the older the child gets, assuming that he or she has demonstrated good decision making in the past. When your children make wise choices, they get favorable results. When they make poor choices, they experience unfavorable outcomes. By interacting with them in this manner, you avoid the need to punish them and, instead, teach them self-discipline: How to make good choices and behave appropriately when no one is around to threaten punishment.

Let's look at another example of how this approach works. Johnny, age 8, has been assigned the task of taking the garbage out on Tuesday and Friday mornings by 7:30. Johnny also wants to go shopping at the mall for a new pair of sneakers this weekend. What do you do? You could wait for Johnny to not take the garbage out, at which point you could anger yourself about his poor performance, punish him for two weeks by grounding him, and then hope that he makes the connection between his poor performance and the punishment you have imposed. Or, you could propose this option:

"Johnny, everyone has been assigned chores to do around the house. Your chore is to make sure the garbage is out front on Tuesdays and Fridays no later than 7:30 in the morning. It's now 7:15. Have you had a chance to get the garbage out yet?"

"No, I've been too busy."

"That's okay, it's just that I remember that you wanted me to take you to the mall this weekend to get a new pair of sneakers."

"Yeah, I still want to do that!"

"This will be our understanding. If you get the garbage out on time every day this week, I will assume that means you still want me to take you to the mall for your sneakers. If you don't get the garbage out on time every day this week, then I'll assume you've *chosen* for me *not* to take you to the mall this weekend. I'll wait to see which choice you make."

The manner in which this situation is set up is perfectly consistent with the idea presented throughout this book that you cannot control other people, including your children. One way you acknowledge this reality is by placing the choice squarely in the hands of the person who really is in control of making it, in this case Johnny.

Johnny also learns the important life lesson that all choices have consequences. I am convinced that the greatest gift parents and teachers can give children is the ability to function fully in the real world when that time comes. You and I have to experience the consequences of our choices, so why shouldn't our children? The sooner they learn the connection between choices and consequences, the sooner they will move toward becoming self-disciplined.

Every morning it was the same. The child would head for the door to catch the school bus with his mother running close behind, angering herself and demanding that he put his jacket on. "What can I do to get him to put his jacket on? We go through this every day!" she said. I suggested that she let him experience the natural consequences of his decision not to wear a jacket and to see how he responded. The next day the child headed for the door without his jacket. Rather than chasing after him, his mother simply wished him a good day at school. As he got outside, he quickly realized that he was cold. He went inside, found his jacket and put it on. Ah, the power of natural consequences!

By having Johnny make the choice, you take yourself out of the position of being the mean, bad parent. In the past, if Johnny didn't get the garbage out on time every day and you punished him by not taking him to get his new sneakers, he would likely condemn you, "I hate you! You won't let me have anything! It's because of you that I have to wear these ratty old sneakers to school!" This new way of handling his discipline allows you to point out that, "Johnny, when you chose not to take the garbage out on time this week that meant you also chose not to get the sneakers." Enough said.

Inherent in the notion of natural consequences is the possibility that the child will choose unwisely and experience some form of psychological or physical discomfort because of that choice. This means there will times when a parent or teacher needs to make the conscious decision to step back, allowing the child to make the wrong choice and to feel the pain associated with that decision. Some adults simply cannot tolerate the notion of children experiencing the discomfort that attaches to making an unwise choice.

To help parents and teachers understand why it is crucial to allow this process to unfold naturally, I always end my seminars with the following story:

How many of you have ever seen the movie Shadowlands? *It is the story of the life of the theologian C. S. Lewis as portrayed by Anthony Hopkins. In the story, Lewis goes around Europe delivering what I refer to as his 'stump speech.' The speech goes something like this. Lewis likens God to a great sculptor. Just like a sculptor in this world takes hammer and chisel in hand, and begins to sculpt a piece of stone until the beautiful piece of art within is revealed, so is God like a great sculptor. We are the pieces of stone. When God takes hammer and chisel in hand, and begins to sculpt us, we feel* **pain**. *But it is only through the experience of pain that we are finally formed as the beautiful pieces of art that God has planned for each of us. To prevent children from experiencing the pain that grows out of* *natural consequences is to interfere with God's sculpting. Your task as a parent or teacher is not to prevent the pain; it is to help the child* **learn** *from the pain.*

One last thought on the topic of punishment. As you know, punishment is designed to decrease certain behaviors. Rewards are designed to increase certain behaviors. As a parent or teacher, understand that rewarding desired behavior is always more powerful than punishing undesirable behavior. Rather than looking for bad behaviors to punish, start spending more time looking for good behaviors to reward. My mother used to tell me, "You draw more flies with honey than you do with vinegar." Become one of those few parents who is good at giving out the honey, rather than being like most parents who are experts only at dispensing the vinegar. Your children will thank you!

Some Controversial Final Thoughts On Parenting

Parents and teachers harbor a number of beliefs about children that are guaranteed to produce anger. Two such beliefs are, "Children must love, respect and obey me," and, "they must always be grateful for the sacrifices I make on their behalf." When children are not as loving as you think they *must* be, or when they don't obey as you think they *should*, or when they are not as grateful for your sacrifices as they *ought to be*, you will make yourself very angry.

Challenging these anger-producing assumptions requires you to undertake that unnatural process of questioning your beliefs. "Where is it written that my children must love me, must obey my every command, and must be appreciative of everything I do for them?" The answer, obviously, is that none of these commands is written anywhere except in your head. Would your relationships with your children be better if they were more loving, obedient and grateful? Absolutely. But must they treat you that way? Regretfully not.

Along the lines of the belief that children must treat their parents and teachers in the above manner is the belief that parents must like and love their children equally. Like other unexamined, oft-repeated beliefs, no one dares subject this belief to review lest they be labeled a bad parent. Unfortunately, the belief that parents must like and love their children equally is a fiction. Think about it for a moment. If the belief, "All parents must like and love their children equally" were true in the real world, that would mean that every parent loved and liked every child, and did so perfectly equally!

Operating from this belief creates a breeding ground for feelings of guilt (a product of "shoulding-on" yourself rather than "shoulding-on" others). The real fact is that not all children are alike, and not all children are equally easy to raise. Whether you accept this reality or not is immaterial. The fact remains that we gravitate toward people who share our own likes and dislikes, whose temperaments are similar to our own, and whose way of seeing the world maps most closely onto our own worldview. Put simply, we like people who are most like ourselves.

To the extent that your child possesses a pleasant temperament, enjoys the things you enjoy, and views things in ways that are consistent with your own values, you will like and love him or her more. To the extent that your child possesses a difficult temperament, rejects the things you enjoy, and views things in ways that are antithetical to what you value, your liking and love for him or her will suffer. Expecting that you would experience great liking and love for a child under the latter conditions is not realistic.

*In my late 20s, my mother and I sat in her kitchen and had one of those rare conversations that "clears the air" for all time regarding a variety of topics. I recall angrily accusing her of preferring my brother to me when we were growing up because, as I had always heard, she **should** have treated us both the same! Her candid answer took me by surprise. "You're right, Brad, I did favor your brother when you were growing up but you have to remember that, from the moment you were born, you were a pretty difficult person to be around. Where Roger was quiet, you were loud. Where Roger was easygoing, you were demanding. If you are to be honest, you were a pain in the butt growing up and your brother wasn't. Now do you understand why I liked Roger better than you?"*

In the next chapter I discuss in detail the "fallacy of unconditional love." Let me anticipate that discussion by saying that granting children unconditional love is just as problematic, if not more so, as granting it to an adult. Unconditional love given to children teaches them that there is nothing they can do within the context of the parent-child relationship that can destroy that bond. *Love always needs to be conditional, even for children!*

CHAPTER SIX

REAPING WHAT YOU SOW: THE EFFECT OF ANGER ON YOUR RELATIONSHIPS

L ike an emotional tornado, anger leaves nothing but destruction and pain in its wake. When someone you love has psychological problems, such as depression or severe anxiety, your initial reaction is stand beside that person as he or she works to resolve their distress. That's not the way it works with anger. For most of us, exposure to chronically angry people results in our doing everything possible to avoid them. Empathizing with an angry person is almost impossible, as much of our time and energy is dedicated to planning our escape.

Nothing exposes your personal strengths and weakness as completely as committing yourself to an intimate relationship with another human being. Because relationships are central to the human experience, and because the level of personal vulnerability is so great, relationships are ripe with opportunities for personal growth, as well as fraught with the potential for despair. For most failed intimate relationships, anger plays a prominent role.

In my first book, I made the following observations:

Though I am often asked to counsel couples having difficulty managing anger within the context of their marriage, I no longer facilitate this type of therapy. I learned rather early on that, by the time a pro-

foundly angry couple decides to seek help, it is usually too late to salvage their relationship. Someone once told me that it takes the average client two years to seek treatment for psychological problems. If the same holds true for couples, that means they have spent those two years locked in angry accusations and non-stop arguments before ever entering my office. While I respect colleagues courageous enough to wade into this messy situation, I do not share their generally hopeful view concerning marital therapy in general, and I am even less sanguine about marital therapy with profoundly angry couples.

Needless to say, these comments did not win me any friends among those who conduct marital therapy! One woman wrote saying how much she had enjoyed my first book, but then noted that she couldn't recommend it to others because I held out so little hope for rescuing marriages damaged by anger. She asked me to reconsider my position in any future writings. Now the time has come to do just that.

Why intimate relationships fail with the frequency they do, and what roles anger plays in those failures, has long been of interest to me. After much reflection, I have come to view anger not necessarily as the cause of the destruction of these relationships, but as the most prominent symptom of the underlying cause. While it can certainly undermine and even accelerate the demise of an intimate relationship, anger is usually the emotional expression of a more fundamental problem. The question then becomes, "What is the fundamental problem that leads certain relationships to fail?" Relationships that are destined to fail—relationships that degenerate into a vicious downward spiral of anger, bitterness and resentment—do so because the persons entering into them *never shared the same personal philosophy.*

You'll recall that personal philosophies are the organized sets of beliefs you have concerning how the world should be and how people you encounter in the world should behave. Your personal philosophy guides your interactions with the world. Some of the beliefs that make up your personal philosphy are more important to you than others. For example, you may believe that Japanese automobiles are superior to American cars. Like your other beliefs, you automatically grant this belief the status of truth. If someone were to challenge this belief you would certainly offer all the data you could to support your position but, if their data were more persuasive, you would likely be open to changing your belief. Altering this belief doesn't cost you anything that is of personal significance, nor does it compel you to re-examine any of the other beliefs making up your personal philosophy. We might call these "flexible" beliefs.

Not all beliefs, however, are flexible. Some beliefs reflect values that are at the very core of your personal philosophy. Core beliefs underpin and influence all of your other beliefs. One way of envisioning the notion of core beliefs is to imagine an onion with many separate layers. As the layers are peeled away, you arrive at the core—that part of the onion that cannot be reduced any further. So, too, do you have many different "layers" of beliefs concerning yourself, others and the world in general.

Because core beliefs are central to your sense of self they are *very resistant to change*. This resistance to change is perfectly understandable. Change requires time, effort and energy. It means moving out of the default comfort zone you know so well, into a discomfort zone where everything is new and nothing is sure anymore. Most people prefer a comfortable level of discomfort to the prospect of change.

Even more importantly, changing core beliefs means that every belief associated with that core belief also needs to be rewritten. The task of rewriting beliefs associated with our core beliefs is monumental. It's akin to changing the first line of code in a computer program and then having to alter all subsequent lines of code in order to accommodate that change. For these reasons you will, as a rule, vigorously avoid changing your core beliefs.

Core beliefs develop around a number of areas of our lives. In his no-nonsense book on relationships titled *The Three Faces Of Love*, Paul Hauck, Ph.D., discusses areas of conflict that couples frequently encounter. While Hauck does not label them core beliefs, the areas he identifies are those around which we tend to develop core beliefs. Those areas include, but are not limited to, how money will be spent within the context of the relationship, what role children will play, how spiritual matters will be dealt with, the relative importance of work vs. play, the need for socializing and, lastly, the importance of sex in the relationship.

What happens when parties to a relationship do not share core beliefs? Imagine a scenario where a couple differs in the core belief of how to handle the family's finances. The husband works in construction while the wife remains at home with their two young children. Because the husband is the sole income producer, he believes that he is entitled to spend his income any way he desires. As a consequence he purchases a variety of "toys," including a fancy pick-up truck, a fishing boat and a motorcycle. For her part, the wife is expected to pay all the bills out of the money he decides to give her at the end of the week. When she asks for money, he accuses her of "nagging him."

One way of viewing this problem is that the individuals don't share the same core beliefs concerning how family resources are to be used. The husband's core beliefs emphasize that, since he earns the money, he can do whatever he wants with it. His needs come first and everyone else's come second. The wife's core beliefs view money as a family resource that should be devoted to meeting the basic needs of the family first, especially the children, and then using whatever is left over for purchasing "toys."

What will happen to this relationship is perfectly predictable. Core beliefs, as we discussed earlier, are highly resistant to change. As the wife becomes increasingly aware of the implications of living according to her husband's core beliefs, she subtly encourages him to abandon those beliefs and to adopt beliefs similar to her own. When her subtle efforts fail, as they almost always will, she becomes more strident until finally she is demanding that he view the area of family finances the same way she does. When he doesn't comply with her demand, she makes herself very angry.

From the husband's perspective, his wife's demand that he alter his core beliefs in this area is viewed as an effort to control him. You have learned how people respond when they perceive others are trying to control them. In this case, rather than moving toward her in a spirit of compromise, he digs in his heels, becomes less likely to compromise, and actually moves away from her psychologically. "Why should I be the one to compromise?" he asks himself. "If she would see things my way, we wouldn't have these problems." So he now tries to get her to change her core beliefs. Subtly, at first, but when his subtle efforts fail, he becomes more strident until finally he is demanding that she view the area of family finances the same way he does. When she doesn't comply with his demand, he makes himself very angry. The end result is a nightmare-like existence characterized by a downward spiral of interpersonal strife, conflict and anger.

The anger found in so many intimate relationships is ultimately the result of two factors. The first is the couple's failure to share core beliefs. *The second is related to the demand made by both of the parties that the other change his or her core beliefs.*

If you don't believe that the vast majority of the conflict and anger found in intimate relationships is due to conflicting core beliefs simply ask yourself the following question, "Would our marriage be better if my wife and I were on the same page regarding how money should be spent, how the children should be disciplined, and whether or not our family should attend church this Sunday?" The answer, obviously, is "yes."

> *When people ask me how long I dated my wife, my response is always the same, "I never dated my wife, I **interviewed** her for three years!"*

For those individuals reading this book who are contemplating entering into an intimate relationship, it is imperative that you take the time (and that can mean years) to get to know your potential partner's core beliefs. If you share the same core beliefs, you can be relatively certain that there will be little anger and conflict in your life together. If your prospective partner does not share your core beliefs and values, then it is better to "bite the bullet" and move on until you find someone who does. Trust me, if this is the only advice in this book that you follow, you will thank me one day!

> *Alice entered my office and began telling me about her marriage to Bob. She recounted how the first year had been total bliss. She could not have been happier and it seemed that they never disagreed about anything. Then, during the second year of their marriage, "Bob began to change." Where once there had been harmony, now there was discord. As a psychologist, I must believe that people are capable of changing. But I also know that elements of a person's basic outlook on the world are highly resistant to change. The chances of Bob changing as drastically as his wife implied were rather remote. That Alice*

had not done a very good job of learning about Bob's core beliefs during their brief courtship was much more likely. What seemed like a change in her husband was most likely his "true self" all the while. If only she had taken the time to get to know that true self.

Returning now to the question of whether or not there is much hope of rescuing marriages where anger is the emotional expression of the conflict growing out of differing core beliefs, my original answer remains fundamentally unchanged. The relationship could be salvaged if:

- the couple recognizes *early on* that there are conflicting core beliefs;

- they understand that differences in core beliefs don't make one person right and the other wrong, just different; and,

- each party is open to exploring and modifying aspects of their respective core beliefs so that they are more aligned with one another.

Under these conditions I believe that the relationship can be salvaged. These are big "ifs," however, and my overall sense remains that most couples are unwilling to make these types of compromises—even if that means ending the relationship.

When anger has damaged a relationship, and the anger is not the result of profound differences surrounding core beliefs, there are techniques you can apply to help rebuild those relationships. Before discussing those techniques, a cautionary note needs to be sounded. Not all relationships can, or even should, be rebuilt. Just because you have changed by becoming less angry does not mean that others must reopen their lives to you.

For some relationships, the depth and breadth of the damage caused by anger is too great to overcome. In those cases, the only option available is to continue working on letting go of your anger and to operate from a stance of sadness over the permanent loss of the relationship. In all cases, the best you can do is make a sincere effort to demonstrate how you have changed and then hope that the other person is willing to try again. Despite your desire to control the outcome, the ultimate decision of whether or not to resume the relationship remains with the person who has received your anger. As a friend once told me, "Only the injured can forgive."

Successful relationships are not the product of secret factors that can only be learned from studying at the feet of highly paid therapists. Successful relationships are the result of keeping in mind certain basic principles, the most important of which I refer to as the "T-Account Principle."

THE T-ACCOUNT PRINCIPLE:
HEALTHY VS. PATHOLOGICAL LOVE

We touched briefly on the idea of unconditional love at the end of the last chapter. By definition, unconditional love is love independent of external factors. This is the supposed ideal form of love because it is love "with no strings attached." How many times have you heard someone say that they were searching for a mate who would love them unconditionally? "I want someone who accepts me just the way I am!" How many times have you heard a parent remark that they love their child unconditionally? I strongly suggest that while the notion of unconditional love may be relevant in terms of God's relationship with His people, it is not relevant, nor even helpful, for this notion to be part of one human being's relationship with another.

When working with women who had been abused by their husbands I always asked why they remained in the marriage. The almost universal response was, "Because I love him." When asked for their *definition* of love, the client would look at me as if I were crazy. "My definition of love? Why love is just, ah, love. It's what I feel toward my husband regardless of what he does to me. I love him unconditionally." To believe in unconditional love is to establish the preconditions for a pathological, or sick, type of love. Affording anyone, much less someone who is abusing you, unconditional love is akin to giving him or her *carte blanche* to continue the abuse.

Don't be naïve, and don't delude yourself. Healthy relationships are built upon the simple premise that *we love people who do things for us that we value.* From this perspective, our love for others is, in all respects, conditional. What this statement lacks in romance and fantasy, it more than makes up for in truth and reality. The only way out of an unhealthy relationship based on unconditional love is to live according to the "T-Account Principle" which is based very much on a belief in *the importance of conditional love.*

In accounting, the most basic technique for recording transactions is called a T-Account. Just as its name implies, this type of account has a line across the top and line down the middle—just like the letter T. On one side of the mid-line is written the word "Debits" and on the other side of the mid-line is written the word "Credits." Debits are withdrawals from the account, while credits are additions or deposits. In healthy relationships, the parties have clearly drawn mental "T-Accounts" where they track the things of value that their partner does for them (credits), along with those things they do not value (debits). As the credit side of the account grows, so grows their love for their partner. As the debit side of the account mounts, their love diminishes.

When I suggest this form of mental accounting to clients who believe in unconditional love, they scoff and declare my view of love and relationships to be unromantic, selfish or even self-centered. They act as if there were something inherently wrong with looking out for one's own well being within the context of a loving relationship. Since schooling as a psychologist involves training in the scientific method, I usually invite the skeptical client to test out my theory by undertaking the following simple experiment: After our session ends, they are to go home and tell their partner to stop doing those things for them that they value. No more breakfast in bed. No more foot rubs at the end of a long day. Nothing! This embargo on making deposits in the relationship is to continue for the indefinite future.

If their belief in unconditional love is true, they should report no decline in their feelings of love for their partner upon returning to my office at some future date. Based on my belief in conditional love, however, I would predict a rather noticeable reduction in their feelings of love toward their partner—and fairly quickly! Though I firmly believe my hypothesis would be proven correct, no client has ever accepted my suggestion to perform this experiment. When you stop doing for your partner the things he or she values, his or her love for you will depart on the same gossamer wings that once delivered it.

BUILDING RELATIONSHIPS VIA DEPOSITS AND WITHDRAWALS

Stephen Covey and I agree that loving relationships involve exchanging things of value between partners, as well as some means for keeping track of those exchanges. In his book *The Seven Habits of Highly Effective People,* Covey introduces the notion of an "Emotional Bank Account" whereas I prefer the metaphor of a T-Account.

If healthy relationships take into account on a series of credits and debits, and anger is the primary means by which you make withdrawals from the accounts you have established with others, then the most pressing question becomes, "Having let go of my anger, how do I start making deposits in my relationships by doing things for others that they value?"

Using the techniques you have learned for letting go of anger is the necessary first step in rebuilding relationships. By letting go of anger you shift your attention from the debit (withdrawal) side of the ledger to the credit side. Rather than constantly worrying about making withdrawals, you can focus your attention on making new deposits.

For Covey, the necessary first step in making deposits involves *understanding what the other person values.* Without truly understanding the other person, how can you know what he or she values and considers to be a deposit? We often assume that what we perceive of as a deposit is what the other person also considers a deposit. Let's say you love golf, and receiving a dozen golf balls from your wife for your birthday constitutes a deposit on her part. Suppose your wife hates golf and you give her a dozen golf balls for her birthday. Have you made a deposit? Absolutely not! As a matter of fact, you've almost certainly made a withdrawal. The only reliable way to find out what another person values is by asking them.

In relationships you quickly learn that, as Covey says, *the little things become the big things.* Putting the toilet seat down, putting the cap back on the toothpaste, cleaning the hair out of the sink, are all little in the grand scheme of things. But if your partner deems them to be important, every time you fail to do one of these little things you make a big withdrawal. Conversely, each time you perform one of these little acts of kindness you make a sizeable deposit.

Val is slow to awaken in the morning. Her morning ritual involves drawing her bath and then, while the tub is filling, pouring herself a glass of soda. Early on in our marriage she asked if I would bring her soda to the bathroom since she was running late. Since that day, almost without fail, she is greeted each morning with a glass of amber liquid on the edge surrounding the bath. A big thing? Certainly not. But enough to constitute a significant deposit on my part.

Another way to make deposits involves *keeping the promises you make to others*. Put simply, keeping a commitment or promise is a major deposit; breaking a promise or commitment is a major withdrawal. If you don't believe me, promise a child a trip to the zoo and then break that promise. Can you think of a more significant withdrawal than making a promise to someone and then not keeping that promise? I recommend only making those promises that you are confident of keeping.

When you enter a new relationship there is always a "honeymoon" period. During this time everything your partner does is considered a deposit and it's almost inconceivable that there would ever be any conflicts, or withdrawals, in the relationship. It is inevitable, however, that there will be withdrawals and many will center on the *expectations* each party brings to the relationship. Allowing expectations to remain unclear establishes the conditions necessary for painful withdrawals. *Clarifying your expectations of others* positions you to make important deposits.

A friend and I were discussing the events leading up to our respective marriages. My friend recounted how he and his girlfriend had dated for an extended period of time during which he had felt increasingly close to her. If the relationship continued on course, they would surely contemplate marriage. As I listened to his story we came to the point where he said, "As we discussed getting married I told her, 'Listen, this may sound terrible, but I don't like children and, if we get married, you need to know that I don't want to have any children. If kids are important to you, then this relationship is probably not going to work.' " I was shocked by his candor and recalled thinking to myself, "What a jerk! How could he say that to her?"

Gradually, however, my reaction changed. You see, my friend was aware of his dislike of children and he was certain that his position would not change with marriage. His core belief and expectation was that there would be no children born of this relationship. Imagine what would have happened if my friend had married this woman without ever discussing his views on children? It would have been a disaster, and possibly a withdrawal large enough to end their marriage. Clarifying expectations takes considerable courage because, as in this case, it might have meant losing a relationship my friend valued greatly. Difficult to do? Yes. But well worth it in the long run.

When assessing whether or not relationships will be relatively free of anger, I am reminded of the commercials for Fram oil filters. A mechanic holds a filter in his hand and says, "You can pay me $10 now to change your oil and filter or (and the camera pans to an engine in pieces) you can pay me $1,000 later to rebuild your engine."

The notion of paying a little bit up front, in order to avoid a much larger payment down the road, is good advice for anyone entering into an intimate relationship. Getting to know your potential partner's core beliefs and expectations up front, and then deciding whether or not they are consistent with your own, can save you much anger, pain and heartache down the road. You can pay a little now or a lot later. It's your choice.

You will make mistakes (withdrawals) in your relationships. When they occur, *a timely and sincere apology* can transform a withdrawal into a deposit. Few things make a more important deposit than an apology from the heart. Psychologically weak people are incapable of apologizing because, in their eyes, that means they made a mistake. Acknowledging your mistakes takes considerable strength and courage. In addition to being timely and sincere, your apology must also include a commitment to the other person, and yourself, to work on not making the same withdrawal (mistake) in the future. Listen to what people say, but *trust* what they do. Words of apology, without corresponding behavioral changes, are meaningless.

Improving relationships damaged by anger can be accomplished by following these few simple principles. Letting go of your anger is the first step. Believing in conditional love is the second step, followed by finding out what your partner values and then providing it on a regular basis. You'll be amazed how quickly your partner's love for you grows!

IMPROVING COMMUNICATIONS

Once you shift from anger to irritation, you position yourself to move from more aggressive to more assertive behaviors. You also position yourself to go from blaming others for the creation of your emotions and behaviors to accepting personal responsibility. Couples attending our anger management seminars always remark how much their communication improves after they learn and practice the techniques I have outlined for letting go of anger. Why is that?

First, when each party to the relationship learns how to let go of anger, it's only natural that communication will improve. Engaging your partner angrily severs lines of communication because that person responds to your anger by snapping their psychological defenses into place. No matter how valid your point might be, the manner in which it's delivered ensures that the recipient will not give it a fair hearing. By letting go of anger, your behavior changes and your message is more likely to be heard and acted upon by your partner.

Second, since you have been learning that you create your own anger, there is no finger pointing, blaming or scapegoating others for your feelings and resultant behaviors. Each party to the relationship takes responsibility for his or her own thoughts, feelings and behaviors. This is what it means to be truly in control of one's self.

When Val and I anger ourselves with one another, we never say that the other person "made" us angry. We understand that we are always the source of our own anger. That being understood, when angry we first ask for time so each of us can go and challenge our anger-producing beliefs. Once that process has been completed and we have shifted from anger to irritation, we come together to solve the problem between us.

Third, couples that learn these techniques for letting go of anger recognize that they are not so powerful that they can create feelings in one another. If I believe that something I want to discuss with Val would "hurt her feelings" then, chances are, I will remain silent. If, however, I understand that I cannot create Val's feelings, that only she can choose whether or not to upset herself about what I might say, then I am much more likely to discuss potential problems with her.

Accepting responsibility for your own feelings, while allowing your partner to assume responsibility for his or hers, changes communication patterns in dramatic ways!

CHAPTER SEVEN

WHY ARE CHILDREN TODAY SO ANGRY?

Family life is our first school for emotional learning; in this intimate cauldron we learn how to feel about ourselves and how others will react to our feelings; how to think about these feelings and what choices we have in reacting; how to read and express hopes and fears. This emotional schooling operates not just through the things parents say and do directly to children, but also in the models they offer for handling their own feelings and those that pass between husband and wife. Some parents are gifted emotional teachers, others atrocious.

Emotional Intelligence, *Daniel Goleman, Ph.D.*

Many of my seminars end with the audience and me seeking answers to the question, "Why are children today so angry?" Parents, educators and therapists agree that anger is a greater problem for children and adolescents today than it has been in the past. Whether this is true or not is open to debate. Less debatable is that adults appear to be afraid of children and the behaviors they are increasingly capable of engaging in—behaviors that were once unthinkable for someone so tender in age.

If we are to be honest, *no one* knows with certainty why children and adolescents seem angrier today. When I ask seminar participants for their best guesses as to why this might be the case, their responses are remarkably consistent and illuminating. From their perspective, children are angrier because of:

- the breakdown of the nuclear family;

- parents divorcing or parents staying in bad marriages;

- parents not being involved enough or parents being too involved;

- too many activities or not enough activities;

- being too sheltered or growing up too fast; and,

- violence in video games, music and the media in general.

A certain thread binds all of these explanations together. Each of these hypotheses involves explaining the child's emotion (anger) and behavior (aggression) in terms of some external event or series of events. By now you should recognize the linkage these types of explanations establish. This is the A $\overrightarrow{\text{causes}}$ C Connection we discussed earlier; the notion that external events cause our emotions and behaviors.

These explanations are known in psychology as "external attributions," or factors external to the individual that account for their emotions and behaviors. Explaining a child's behavior solely based on external attributions gives the child what type of message? The very powerful message received by the child is that they are not responsible for their own thoughts, feeling and behaviors. In our culture, the absence of responsibility also implies the absence of accountability. If aggression on TV causes the child to behave violently, then the child cannot be held accountable for his or her behavior.

Given this message, is it any wonder that children (and many adults) seem so unwilling to accept responsibility for their actions? We have become a society expert at finding new and clever ways to absolve people of responsibility for their emotions and behaviors. Unfortunately, these types of explanations create a breeding ground for exactly the types of behaviors we, as a society, most abhor.

A theme throughout this book involves holding people accountable for their thoughts, feelings and behaviors. The emphasis is on developing internal attributions for why someone *chooses* to think, feel and behave a certain way. It is valid to question the extent to which children, especially very young children, are in control of their thoughts, feelings and behaviors. Clearly children are capable of learning; the extent to which they can directly manipulate their own thoughts, to achieve different emotional and behavioral outcomes, is less clear. My sense is that very young children, up to age 6-7, mostly mimic the behaviors of the adults around them. In this respect, the external environment is likely to be the most important determinant of the very young child's emotional and behavioral reactions.

As children grow older, and their ability to think abstractly matures, we need to help them understand that, regarding their emotions and behaviors, the external environment becomes less important while the internal, mental world, takes center stage. As the child moves through adolescence, and then into adulthood, I am suggesting the rather radical notion that *the external environment, as a determinant of emotions and behaviors, plays no role whatsoever!* This assertion is perfectly consistent with the notion discussed earlier that life circumstances, in and of themselves, are always meaningless; their meanings being determined by how the individual chooses to think about those circumstances.

POSSIBLE EXPLANATIONS FOR WHY CHILDREN ARE ANGRIER

> *It is human to imitate the habits of those with whom we interact. We inadvertently adopt their interests, their opinions, their values and their habit of interpreting events. Epictetus*

Multiple explanations exist for why children today are angrier. One possibility is that children, especially very young children, observe and imitate the emotional and behavioral responses of their primary caretakers. Like little video cameras, children record how the adults around them deal with life's challenges. Since adults today appear angrier than they have been in the past, their children may be modelling adult emotional and behavioral responses.

Since adults have no conceptual framework for understanding where their own anger comes from, they are poorly positioned to educate their children concerning the origins of this emotion. To the extent that they lack an understanding of where anger comes from, adults teach children the A $\overrightarrow{\text{causes}}$ C Connection; that is, that other people make the child angry. While perpetuating that myth is good for my business, it merely creates the conditions for the next generation of angry children, adolescents and adults. If parents understand that they anger themselves, and then teach that to their children, the intergenerational transmission of anger will most assuredly lessen, if not end completely.

Another possible explanation for the increased anger in children is linked to the fact that, like adults, children also make the erroneous connection that it was their anger that helped them get what they demanded. Recall the mother who came into my office complaining because her son pitched a fit in the middle of Wal-Mart when she refused to buy him a box of expensive cereal. She solved the problem posed by his behavior by purchasing the cereal!

What does the child learn from this situation? He learns that getting angry, and screaming loudly, yields success. Is it any wonder then that this process begins over again when he sees another new cereal on TV? Other than giving into his demands, what responses were available to his mother?

She could sit beside her son whenever he was watching TV and switch off cereal commercials. She could videotape all the TV programs her son watches and then, late at night, edit out all the new cereal commercials, letting him watch the shows on a time delay basis. Or, she could hire a baby sitter each time she needs to go cereal shopping so she doesn't have to worry about him pitching a fit in the store. While certainly lessening her discomfort, none of these options would teach her son self-discipline.

What could she have done differently? I offered her two possible solutions. The next time her son angered himself in the store, she was to kneel beside him and say, "Johnny, I'm sorry you've chosen to upset yourself over not getting the cereal. I'd prefer that you stop yelling and come with me, but if you want to continue screaming, there is really nothing I can do to stop you. If you would like to stay in the aisle and scream, that's fine with me. I'll be back for you in a few minutes." And then walk away.

This approach has three benefits. First, the mother is talking B $\xrightarrow{}$ C to her son when she says, "Johnny, I'm sorry you've chosen to upset yourself over not getting the cereal;" thereby beginning the process of teaching her son that he is responsible for his emotions and behaviors. Second, she is telling her son the behaviors she would prefer, all the while reminding herself that she has no direct control over her son's behavior. This decreases the chance that she will anger herself and either say or do something she later regrets. Third, she forcefully conveys to the child that she will not be held hostage by his poor behavior and will continue with her tasks. Had she chosen this approach, I suspect her son would have quieted down rather quickly.

The other approach involves using what is called a *paradoxical intervention*. A paradoxical intervention involves asking someone to do more of a particular behavior that you really want him or her to stop. Using this approach she could have knelt next to her son and said, "Johnny, what a wonderful screaming voice you have. But I'm sure you can scream louder and carry on even more than that. How about screaming louder for me? Would you do that for me? How about making even more of a fuss? I'll just sit here and we'll see if you can't scream and carry on even more." By asking her son to do more of what it was that she wanted him to stop doing, her son would quickly become confused and give up his screaming. After all, it's no fun screaming if mom isn't going to reward your behavior by upsetting herself.

> *The simple rule here is that upsetting yourself about*
> *poor behavior often rewards poor behavior!*

Key to the success of both of these strategies is the mother's ability to manage her potentially angry response to her son's behavior. By practicing self-discipline, the mother positioned herself to devise a response that solved her problem; at the same time, helping to teach her son self-discipline.

WOW BOX

When you call your child, be prepared that she might not respond to you, or if she does, she might not do what you want her to do. Under these circumstances, it does not help your child for you to become agitated. It should not be in her power to cause you any disturbance.
Epictetus

A developmental factor driving anger in children and adolescents is related to the fact that they are moving through a profoundly egocentric stage in their lives. To be egocentric is to be self-centered, self-important, self-absorbed and *entitled*. There is little room for "others" in the egocentric world of children. Having needs met immediately, without interference, is of paramount concern. Whoever or whatever blocks the attainment of their self-centered goals quickly becomes the object of their anger. Rewarding the egocentric, entitled stance of children and adolescents by giving in to their angry outbursts does not further the goal of teaching them how to live in the World of Is.

In the real world the wishes of others also need to be taken into consideration. In the real world, gratification is almost never immediate. And in the real world, they are not entitled to anything. As a matter of fact, giving in to their anger actually retards their growth. Standing firm in the face of their egocentric, entitled demands requires that you first understand the nature of your own anger and then resist either capitulating or retaliating against your children.

Another possible explanation for the anger expressed by children and adolescents is related to how limited their resources are when compared to those possessed by adults. Children and adolescents are painfully aware of their inability to meet almost all of their basic needs. Ten year-old Sally can't get the keys to the car, drive to McDonald's and buy herself a hamburger. Nor could she pay for the clothes she wears, or for the concert tickets she bought last week. To achieve almost any goal, or acquire almost any material good, she must either enlist, or try coercing, the adults around her. As those adults give in to her angry demands, they reinforce and reward her anger.

Given their limited resources, children and adolescents have less power than the adults around them do. Anger may serve as a means of clawing back some of the power adults have and, in that respect, may be viewed by children and adolescents as a way of leveling the playing field. Anger gives people, including children and adolescents, the sense of being more potent than they really are. In this respect the child's anger may make him or her feel more powerful in dealing with the adult world.

Finally, children and adolescents have a compressed sense of time based upon their limited experiences with the world. They are masters of what others have called "low-frustration tolerance" or LFT. They believe that they must get everything they demand immediately because any delay means waiting for what seems to be an agonizingly long period of time. How often have you told your child that he or she would need to wait until the weekend in order to visit the mall, only to hear the predictably dramatic response, "But I can't wait *that* long!" Tomorrow is an eternity to children, and they will anger and frustrate themselves greatly when they do not get what they demand, when they think they should, must and ought to get it. If you are going to teach your child how to delay gratification, you can expect to deal with their anger.

The Question Of Bullying

Issues surrounding bullying have taken on heightened significance since the occurrence of tragedies at schools in Jonesboro, Arkansas; Pearl, Mississippi; Santee, California and Columbine, Colorado. In each of these cases, angry young men lashed out aggressively against fellow classmates and teachers. Americans were deeply shaken as they contemplated the reality of children killing other children.

Following each event came the same question: "What could cause children to behave so horrifically?" One story I read suggested the following answers:

- unresolved and unrecognized grief issues;

- family systems that foster aggression and condone bullying;

- school systems that allow "boys to be boys;"

- communities that value winning at sports competitions or in the business arena at all cost; and,

- the media teaching children through films, songs and video games that violence and hurtful behaviors are an integral and valued part of society.

What strikes you immediately about these explanations? Each involves an external attribution for the child's behavior. As you will recall, external attributions convey the message that individuals are not responsible for their behaviors. I am simply not comfortable with these types of explanations.

The explanation with which I am least comfortable, however, is the one that has emerged repeatedly as the children who commit these terrible acts are debriefed by the authorities: "Other kids bullied me, and they wouldn't stop. I just couldn't take the teasing any more." While I am offended that the "bullying defense" has become the justification *de jour* for these children, even more problematic is the fact that many adults accept this explanation as sufficient to absolve children of responsibility for their heinous acts.

For most of my life I have been overweight. I was overweight as a child. As a child, I was ceaselessly teased because of my weight. If I had killed every person who ever teased me, my personal history would be littered with dead bodies. Somehow I learned that being teased did not give me carte blanche *to kill others. Wasn't it the same for you?*

What, to this point, has been our culture's response to the problem of bullying and teasing? It has been exactly as I would have predicted: the *wrong* response. The focus has been on changing the external environment within which children function. One idea pursued by the faculty at Columbine High School involved publishing a manifesto requiring that every student and member of the faculty pledge to refrain from any type of teasing. The assumption was that eliminating teasing would eliminate the *cause* of children aggressing towards one another. While I'm sure this made the faculty, students and parents "feel" better, and "feel" as if they were doing something to address the problem, this kind of response is worse than doing nothing because it reinforces the notion that the world will change in order to lessen the victim's discomfort.

For the sake of argument, let's assume that everyone at Columbine agreed to abide by the terms of the no-teasing agreement. And let's further assume that everyone at Columbine who signed the agreement actually lived up to it. What happens when one of these children graduates from high school and goes to college, where no one signed onto this agreement and he is once again subjected to teasing? Or let's assume that no one at college ever teases him. What happens when he goes out into the work world and finds that none of his co-workers bought into this agreement? This approach fails miserably because it doesn't provide the child with the skills he needs to function in the real world—a world where teasing and bullies exist.

148

I do not condone teasing and bullying and, in a perfect world, they would not be problems. Unfortunately, we do not live in a perfect world, nor is the existence of such a world anticipated any time soon. The problem with the response discussed above is that it focuses exclusively on changing the bully. While facilitating a pro-social change in the bully's behavior is certainly worth trying (and is the focus of almost every anti-bullying program), the larger question becomes, "What happens if the bully refuses to change?" By focusing on changing the bully, the victims have chosen to hold themselves psychologically hostage to the willingness of the bully to change: "I will feel better if, and only if, the bully stops teasing me."

Again the question, "But what if the bully chooses not to change?" Though some will label my answer a form of "blaming the victim," you have been learning *there are no victims in this world—only people making choices about how they view their life.* Victimization is not what someone does to you, but something you do to yourself! As I write this section I hear the echoes of an old nursery school rhyme: "Sticks and stones may break my bones, but names can never hurt me." When did we as a culture forget this important truth? Words, in and of themselves, are meaningless. Contrary to the notion of political correctness, words do not have the power to hurt us unless we allow them to do so.

Instead of teaching children that the meanings they assign to words determine whether or not they are hurtful, and that the meanings they assign are a choice they make, we teach them that words have the same physical effect as being hit by a stone or struck by a stick. Not only can sticks and stones break one's bones, so now can the words of a bully. Given what we teach them, is it any wonder that some children react violently to perceived verbal assaults? Crucial to "bullying-proofing" children is helping them understand what is, and is not, true about the power of words.

> *Sticks and stones may break my bones, but names*
> *can never (unless I allow them to) hurt me.*

HELPING ANGRY CHILDREN:
POSSIBLE SOLUTIONS

Before commercial aircraft take off, passengers are instructed about the safety features and procedures for the aircraft. One procedure involves placing an oxygen mask over your face if the cabin loses pressure. When travelling with someone who is either young, old, or ill, whose mask are you instructed to put on first—yours or the person's you are travelling with? The correct answer is to put yours on because if you do not take care of yourself first you will be of little help to the other person. The same principle applies when trying to help your children deal with anger. First you must address your own anger before you are in a position to help them deal with theirs.

Bookstore shelves are overflowing with clever titles that focus on teaching adults techniques for getting children to alter their behavior. What this book adds to this topic is its intense focus on the need for adults to discipline themselves before attempting to discipline others. The simple message is that *other-discipline before self-discipline doesn't work.*

The technique, or combination of techniques, that works best with a particular child is influenced by a variety of factors: the quality of the adult's relationship with the child (does the child view the adult as someone who inspires trust and respect, who practices what he or she preaches?); the child's cognitive ability (the degree to which the child can think abstractly); and the child's motivation to change. Most books dealing with children are written by behaviorally oriented therapists. Their approach focuses on altering external envi-

150

ronmental factors to change children's behavior. While these techniques work well with very young children, they will become less effective because the internal or mental world becomes a more important determinant of behavior as the child ages. For any change to be truly lasting, the thoughts that drive children's emotions and behaviors must change.

By now you agree that working with children requires that you possess a framework for understanding your own experience of anger. This book gives you that framework. Once in possession of this understanding, you must not only talk the talk, but walk the walk. Especially with very young children, your example is your most powerful teaching tool. Moving toward mastery of your own thoughts, emotions and behaviors gives you the personal integrity and authenticity necessary for you to deal with children.

TECHNIQUES FOR WORKING WITH CHILDREN THAT EMPHASIZE EXTERNAL FACTORS

Children can be trained to pay attention to the physiological cues (such as increased muscle tension, increased heart rate and stomach in knots) and behavioral cues (such as yelling, hitting things and throwing things) that reliably precede their angry outbursts. Teach them to view those cues as "early warning signs" that they are about to explode angrily with all the negative consequences such an explosion entails. Once they have identified the warning signs, teach them the importance of taking a time out from the situation about which they are upsetting themselves.

Structuring a time out is well known to all who work with children. While a time out can be helpful, children in time out must be given a different way to *think* about the situations they have angered themselves about. Brief self-statements like, "Things aren't always fair;" or "Just because my sister hits me doesn't mean I have to hit her back;" or "I don't always have to get what I want, when I want it;" can be rehearsed during the time out to help reduce their anger.

Watch your language carefully, especially around children. *Never* reinforce the notion that other people make them angry. Rather than asking, "Did so-and-so make you angry today?" phrase it, "Did you *choose* to anger yourself over what so-and-so did today?" When you talk A $\overrightarrow{\text{causes}}$ C to children, that is what you teach them. By talking B $\overrightarrow{\text{causes}}$ C, you help children accept responsibility for the creation of their own emotions and behaviors.

It can also be useful to discuss with children how anger has interfered with their lives, especially their important relationships. Most children enjoy relating to their peers and adults. If you can make the direct connection between high levels of anger and aggression and impaired interpersonal relationships, many children will opt to feel less angry.

Introducing the T-Account Principle discussed in Chapter Six can lead to significant changes in how adults and children interact. The beauty of this technique is that it emphasizes the transactional nature of all healthy relationships. It also encourages adults and children to talk directly about those behaviors they consider to be "deposits" and those they view as "withdrawals." By keeping track of this process in a place where all parties can see it, (for instance, on the refrigerator door) family members can constantly track the status of their relationships.

Take advantage of the natural tendency of children to be egocentric by appealing directly to their self-interest. One way to do this is by pointing out that they will get more of the "good stuff" by not getting angry, and less of the good stuff by getting angry. One colleague views children as "little business people." That is, they are constantly seeking ways to get more of what they want from the adults around them. When their non-angry, non-aggressive responses are reinforced, children learn that they get more by responding this way than they did by getting angry and behaving poorly.

Finally, although it requires that they work against their egocentric tendencies, find ways to help children learn to empathize with others. Empathy is the ability to put oneself in the place of another. One way to do this is by either videotaping or audiotaping the child's angry outbursts and then playing the tape back. Like adults, children often have no idea how they appear to others when they are angry. This technique allows them to know exactly how their tantrum appears to others.

TECHNIQUES FOR WORKING WITH CHILDREN THAT EMPHASIZE INTERNAL FACTORS

When possible, help children use humor to challenge their anger-producing beliefs. This is not the same as having them make fun of those beliefs. Rather, get children to articulate their beliefs and then ask them to step back and evaluate how realistic they are. If you can get them to act out dramatically their anger-producing beliefs, like I do while driving, so much the better. The object of the exercise is to get them to recognize how foolish their anger-producing beliefs are so that they will abandon them.

One of the most powerful lessons you can teach children grows out of the distinction between the "World of Should" and the "World of Is" as found in Chapter Four. Children need to learn that there is a difference between the way they think the world should be, and the way it really is. This gives you an opportunity to discuss the twin notions of fairness and unfairness.

Children have very strongly held views about what constitutes fair and unfair treatment. Help them understand that the belief "life *must* be fair" has no support in your experience and that life is sometimes unfair. When confronted by unfairness, the only freedom they have is the freedom to choose how they respond to that unfairness. Will they anger themselves, thereby increasing the likelihood of doing or saying something that causes them further problems? Or will they let go of their anger in the face of the unfairness, thereby motivating them to find a way to redress their concerns?

Being treated fairly or unfairly is something out of our control. How we choose to respond to such treatment is something completely within our control. Life offers us no guarantees.

Teach children that emotions are not things that just happen to them, over which they have no control, but are products of how the child *thinks* about life circumstances. By using teaching stories they can come to understand this concept. Ed Nottingham, Ph.D., is fond of telling the following story to his clients. For your purposes, simply substitute your child or adolescent for the client. Ed asks his client to imagine standing in line at McDonald's after a particularly unpleasant day at work (substitute school for work). The client is very tired and the line ahead is painfully long and slow moving. The client looks up at the menu when, all of a sudden, there is a sharp tap in the middle of his back.

Without turning around, he begins getting angry. Thoughts like, "He *should* be more considerate!" and "He *should* watch what he is doing!" begin filling the client's head. The tapping continues for another minute or two until the client has so angered himself that he turns around to "let the other guy have it." Then he realizes that the person tapping him on the back is blind and is doing so by mistake. Given this new information, the client's thoughts and then feelings change. Anger is replaced with feelings of shame and perhaps even guilt.

But where did the anger go? The person kept on tapping, yet the client's anger vanished because he changed how he *thought* about being tapped. There are countless stories you can use to illustrate the point that changing the way you think about something leads to changes in how you feel about it. Recounting specific instances of how your feelings changed because your thinking changed would be a powerful lesson for your young listeners.

> *A grandfather was talking to his grandson about how he felt. He said, "I feel as if I have two wolves fighting in my heart. One wolf is the vengeful, angry and violent one. The other is the loving, compassionate one." The grandson asked him, "Which will win the fight in your heart?" The grandfather answered, "The one I feed."*

When you are angry at a child's behavior, your behavior will reflect that anger. Yelling and screaming doesn't work because the child will view your behaviors as an effort at control and resist you. Using the tools that allow you to shift from anger to irritation positions you to approach your child in a manner that makes it more likely that he or she will at least hear what you are asking. Rather than yelling, screaming and telling the child how angry you are about a certain behavior, talk to the child out of your *disappointment* in the behavior.

Think about your own experience as a child. What was worse—having your mother or father stand before you, yelling, screaming and demanding that your behavior change—or having your parents sit calmly next to you as they told you exactly how disappointed they were by your behavior? Almost everyone agrees that parental disappointment was a more powerful motivator for change than parental anger and disapproval. Talking to children out of your disappointment makes you very powerful.

Lastly, help them understand that there is no such thing as unconditional love—including the love between a parent and child. Needless to say, this is a very controversial notion and one which most women (including my wife) have trouble embracing. While the love between you and your child may be qualitatively different than the love between you and your wife, or between you and a friend, the need to establish boundaries or limits for the love of your child is just as important as in your other relationships.

It is understandable that the amount of latitude or credit you might grant your child is far greater than what you might grant others. That there would be no outermost limit to your love, such that the child would not fear crossing that boundary, is the major problem. Children need to understand that while your love for them is flexible to a degree, it is not infinitely flexible and is capable of breaking beyond repair based on their behavior. *Love, especially with your child, always needs to be conditional.*

CHAPTER EIGHT

ANGER AND YOUR PAST: COMING TO GRIPS WITH ABUSE, TRAUMA AND LOSS

The last of the human freedoms is to choose one's attitude.

—Victor Frankl

T he wife of a prospective client called to arrange therapy for her husband regarding his explosive anger. She began the conversation by noting that he had changed during their three-year marriage and had become verbally abusive. In addition to her concerns about whether his verbal aggression would escalate into a physical confrontation, she expressed concern that her young son would grow up having a "temper like his father."

As we discussed her husband's previous failed efforts at treatment, she offered the following observation, "I think what really makes my husband angry is how he was treated as a child. His father was a very angry man who verbally and psychologically abused all his children." At that point I stopped and asked her, as I am now asking you, to consider the following observations.

Therapy, because it appears shrouded in mystery and is an exercise relatively few people participate in, is full of myths. One myth requires that successful therapy involve an exploration and resolution of past issues. I am constantly amazed by clients who, upon entering my office, look around for the couch they are supposed to lie down on while staring at the ceiling as they describe their terrible childhood. This remains the stereotypical view of therapy.

Numerous techniques for dealing with the full range of human psychological problems do not require a retreat into the past in order to find solutions in the present. You have been learning one of those techniques, known as cognitive therapy, throughout this book. The past can influence your present; but for the woman to attribute her husband's *current* anger to events occurring in his childhood is both unhelpful and untrue.

It is unhelpful because it is not possible to do therapy in the past; one can only work therapeutically in the present and the future. The wife would have been more accurate if she had said, "Bob's father was a very angry man who verbally and psychologically abused all his children; and *Bob continues angering himself* over that treatment to this very day." Even though the activator, in this case the abuse, may have occurred in the past, Bob's anger is always in the present based on how he thinks about that past activator. While it is impossible to edit the past, it is possible to change how you think and feel about events from your past.

Throughout this book you have been learning that you create your anger in the present based on how you think about current activators. Simply because an activator occurred in the past does not change how your anger in the present is formed. You have the tools to let go of anger, whether the activator is a current problem or one you faced in the distant past. Use your tools!

ANGER IN RESPONSE TO ABUSE

Anger is where you take the poison,
then wait for the other person to die.

That persons suffer sexual, emotional and physical abuse is without question. How best to understand and treat abuse is the source of some controversy. For the past 30 years, our society has glorified those who view themselves as "victims" of abuse. In the process of glorifying victimhood, an entire industry developed which was designed to help these individuals, when in fact, it served only to perpetuate their victim status.

The treatment of past abuse (physical, emotional or sexual), as prescribed by the "victim industry," dictates that victim's first "get in touch" with their anger. From this perspective victims are perfectly justified in being angry and must acknowledge the anger before *feeling* better. Once victims acknowledge their righteous anger, the victim industry requires that they "confront" their abusers and demand that the abusers take responsibility and then apologize for their actions. This approach is fraught with problems.

First, angering yourself in the present, over an activator that took place years ago, is a waste of your precious time and limited psychological resources. The anger you produce today in no way alters the past and serves only to make you miserable in the present.

Second, what happens if, after confronting the abuser, that person denies the abuse or refuses to apologize? What then? You have in essence tied your *feeling* better to the abuser accepting responsibility for certain behaviors. But persons who abuse others don't usually "play nice" or "play by the rules." Waiting for the abuser to acknowledge their actions and apologize may mean waiting a lifetime. Are

159

you prepared to hold your happiness hostage until the abuser "does the right thing?"

Third, as long as you believe that your father, mother, aunt, uncle, brother, sister or neighbor makes you angry because of what they did to you 30 years-ago, who is in control of your emotions? The very person who committed the abuse. While you may not like hearing this, your current anger simply perpetuates the earlier abuse. As the introduction to this section states, in this case *anger is where you take the poison, and then wait for the abuser to die.*

> *Michelle's parents were both addicted to drugs. They would "give" their daughter to dealers in exchange for drugs. Even now I am shocked at the scope of the abuse she experienced. At the end of our work together she said something I've never forgotten.*
>
> *"When we first began working together I was so angry," she said. "Whenever I thought about the abuse, my anger became so great that I almost couldn't breathe. It was like someone was grabbing my hair and holding my head under water. I was gasping for air. Now that our time has come to an end I recognize that the physical abuse ended over 20 years ago, and that since that time, because of my anger, it was really my own hand holding my head under water."*

When experiences like abuse shatter our beliefs about how the world should, must and ought to be, we experience anger. What needs to happen for someone who has been abused to let go of anger? It is crucial to understand that the core anger-producing belief when dealing with abuse is always, "This *shouldn't* have happened to me." The most powerful response to this statement is, "Help me understand *why the abuse shouldn't have happened to you.*"

> *Sylvia is 41 years old. I had met her while doing a rotation on an inpatient psychiatric unit. She was contacting me now because, "No*

one else will see me. You are my last hope to deal with my anger." Ten minutes into the session I recalled the details of the problem that led her to seek inpatient treatment. An older brother had sexually abused her for many years. While he currently enjoyed considerable professional success and social prestige, she languished in a series of low-paying jobs and had few, if any, friends.

Though the actual abuse stopped more than 25 years ago, she continued harboring feelings of profound anger toward him because he steadfastly refused to acknowledge that it had taken place. As the session came to an end I suggested to Sylvia that, if she were to "get better," she would ultimately need to abandon her anger toward her brother.

Her jet black eyes grew even smaller and she screamed, "You can't possibly expect me not to be angry with my brother for what he did to me! He destroyed my life!" At that point she stormed out of my office and I did not see her again. When a client like Sylvia is allowing anger to destroy her life and is looking for a therapist to "validate" her anger, I refuse to collaborate in that process.

When asked "Why shouldn't this have happened to you?" many clients appear stunned. No one ever thought to ask the victims to question their perceptions of the abuse, or the role they might be playing in perpetuating the abuse. The focus has always been on validating the victim's experience—as if they needed a therapist's validation in order for their experiences to be real! His or her experiences were real, and certainly no reasonable person would argue that point. But the victim's perceptions or beliefs about the abuse need to change for them to let go of their anger.

The "Why shouldn't it have happened to you?" question leads invariably to the following exchange:

Client: "But I didn't do anything to invite or warrant the abuse!"

BPB: "I understand that you didn't do anything to invite or warrant the abuse. So I guess what you are saying is that uninvited, unwarranted things should happen to other people, but not to you?"

Client: "That's not what I am saying at all! Uninvited, unwarranted, unfair things shouldn't happen to anyone!"

BPB: "You're right, and in a perfect world, uninvited, unwarranted, unfair things wouldn't happen to anyone. But you're not here in my office, struggling to let go of your anger, because you are living in a perfect world. You are in my office, struggling to let go of your anger, because *you are living in an imperfect world, all the while demanding that it be perfect.*"

My style of therapy is highly confrontational. Not everyone who has experienced abuse can tolerate this kind of directness. I understand that, and each therapist and client will need to work at their own pace. Whatever pace you work at, however, you will eventually need to address the core anger-producing belief which is always, "This shouldn't have happened to me."

Earlier I suggested that anger, when it is an outgrowth of some form of disrupted relationship, is always a secondary emotion. The primary emotional experience is always hurt, sadness and disappointment. Abuse is the ultimate form of relationship disruption. Once the core anger-producing belief has been addressed and the feelings of anger have lessened, emotions like profound hurt and sadness will arise. These emotions position the client to move toward an acceptance of what took place. With that acceptance may even come the possibility of forgiveness.

Only after letting go of your anger do you position yourself to forgive another. Forgiveness is not a gift you give the transgressor; rather, it *is a gift you give yourself.* Forgiving the abuser allows you to reclaim psychological energy that you had devoted to perpetuating your anger and thus the abuse. Forgiveness allows you to reallocate your energies toward more productive ends—like living without anger in the present and in the future.

ANGER IN RESPONSE TO TRAUMA

The events of September 11, 2001 traumatized a nation. Two days after the event I was scheduled to conduct seminars in Albuquerque and Santa Fe, New Mexico. With flying not an option, my assistant Jeana and I jumped into the car and made the 1,300 mile trip as we listened on the radio as events unfolded in New York and Washington, D.C.

During the final break of the day, a gentleman at the Santa Fe seminar approached and said, "I really needed to hear what you had to say today. But, be honest, even you had to get angry as you watched those planes crash into the World Trade Center. How could anyone not be angry witnessing such a horrible deed?" Having anticipated the question, I was surprised that no one had asked it in the larger session. "My sense is that there are many people in the audience who are wondering the same thing. Would it be okay if I gave my answer to the whole group?" "Sure," he replied and returned to his seat.

When we reconvened, this is what I said, "During the break a gentleman approached and asked if I became angry witnessing the events that occurred in New York and Washington the other day. He went on to state how he didn't think it was possible for anyone to *not* be angry given what happened.

"By now you should appreciate that the most important thing to me is to live according to the philosophy of life I have presented to you today. That personal philosophy views anger as a destructive force that I create for myself based not on life circumstances, but based upon how I choose to view those circumstances.

"The trauma we as a nation collectively experienced, and the anger growing out of those events, is based on the simple belief that these events should not have occurred to us. The question we need to ask ourselves is, 'Where is it written that bad things shouldn't happen to Americans? Are we as a people so special that the evil visited upon other peoples around the world should somehow escape us?' The answer, obviously, is that we are no different than anyone else. We are not *entitled* to live in a world free of risk or evil.

"The most devastating collisions occurring on 9/11 did not involve two planes crashing into the World Trade Centers, or the single plane slamming into the Pentagon. The most devastating collision, between the World of Should and the World of Is, was the one that occurred in the minds of millions of Americans. When those two worlds met on that fateful day, the World of Is prevailed as it always does. Since I do not believe in the notion of a World of Should, I was profoundly saddened by those events, but not angry. Remember, this personal philosophy is not just about letting go of anger over life's small inconveniences, but about letting go of anger even in the face of life's greatest challenges."

ANGER AND LOSS

> **WOW BOX**
>
> *Nothing can be truly taken from us. There is nothing to lose. Inner peace begins when we stop saying of things, "I have lost it" and instead say, "It has been returned to where it came from." Have your children died? They are returned to where they came from. Has your mate died? Your mate is returned to where he or she came from. The important thing is to take great care with what you have while the world lets you have it. Epictetus*

One of the joys of lecturing around the country is that people learn of my work and then correspond with me about their real-life struggles with anger. In one such instance, a woman wrote that she had begun reading the first book and was finding it to be of help. She went on to explain that a disease had been diagnosed in her son. This malady would require ongoing medical attention and inevitably result in his death at a young age.

She wrote that this "bad news" had been received five years earlier and that she was still struggling to get over her anger. I wrote her back and, among other things, suggested that there was no such thing as "bad news;" that news, in and of itself, is neutral and that it was her interpretation that made it "bad." Here is her response:

Dear Dr. Barris, I appreciate your response but have an initial recoiling at the thought that "bad news" is neutral and that it is how I *interpret this that counts. This sounds like something my appreciated therapist might say. I will make a concerted effort in the long haul to gain understanding. I have nothing to lose by disputing notions from my past and embracing these new ideas. If I don't practice and continue learning appropriate ways to think about this situation, **I have everything to lose.***

I understand that this is a difficult notion to grasp, especially as one contemplates the loss of a child. No one ever said that letting go of anger, a process that requires that we transcend our nature, was going to be painless. Here, once again, the core anger-producing beliefs are, "This shouldn't have happened to me!" or "This shouldn't have happened to my son!" or "The story isn't ending like it should. Children should bury their parents, not the other way around!" You have seen these questions repeatedly during the last few sections of this chapter. You know how they need to be answered in order to let go of anger. Now, answer them.

Not long before his death, Arthur Ashe was being interviewed about accidentally contracting HIV from a simple blood transfusion. The reporter inquired, "Don't you ever get angry when you think about how this happened? Don't you ever ask, 'Why did this happen to me?' " Ashe's powerful response, according to the report, sounded something like this: "If I were to get angry and question why this is happening to me now, I would also need to question why I have enjoyed all the blessings I've known in my life. You see, just as I didn't do anything to earn what is happening to me now, I didn't do anything to warrant those blessings, either." It is this philosophical stance towards life that ennobles us in the face of death.

AND IN THE END:
BEING GRATEFUL FOR YOUR ACTIVATORS

As mentioned earlier, Shadowlands *is a movie I frequently recommend to clients who are struggling to meet important life challenges. This remarkable story captures the life of C. S. Lewis as he moves from writing and lecturing about the notions of joy and pain and actually begins experiencing both. Lewis had successfully avoided both of these powerful emotional experiences by steadfastly refusing to love another. That is, until a woman, appropriately enough named Joy, entered his life.*

Shortly after knowing the joy of their marriage pain came as the couple learned that Joy was dying of cancer. Tears of happiness transformed into tears of anger as Lewis demanded to know why God was taking Joy from him. His anger and pain were so great that, at one point, he even questioned his decision to love her at all.

Given the above scenario, why would I suggest to Lewis that, rather than angrily questioning his choice to love a dying Joy, it would be more appropriate for him to experience profound gratitude for their relationship? If her death is viewed as an activator for his anger, why would I suggest that he, in essence, be grateful for her death?

Earlier in the book we discussed gratitude as it relates to entitlement-related forms of anger. Here we discuss the notion of being *grateful* for the activators—the problems—in your life. Admittedly, this is not an easy concept to understand, nor is it easy to put into practice. Activators are the real-life problems we need to solve. Just as those of you who have ever fought in war know that it is one thing to train for battle, and another thing entirely to fight in battle; so, too, is discussing how to respond to life's challenges different from actually meeting those challenges head on. Only by responding to life's real challenges do we understand completely what our capabilities are. This is the nature of life.

By welcoming activators into your life, and then solving the problems they present, you truly learn what you are made of. For C. S. Lewis, the death of Joy served as the most profound activator imaginable for his anger. It shook the very foundations of his world and religious convictions. Yet it was only by mentally struggling with her death that he was able to overcome the beliefs that brought him such anger and pain.

Ultimately, Lewis transformed his anger at Joy's death into sadness, and then once again into joy, by recalling the advice she had given him one afternoon as they huddled in a barn to avoid a pouring rain. Where Lewis, known to his friends as Jack, wanted to avoid the topic of her impending death, Joy knew she had to prepare him for it. "It's not going to last, Jack," she said. "But that doesn't spoil it; it just makes it real. What I'm trying to say is that the pain then is part of the happiness now. That's the deal." Without being willing to experience the pain growing out of her death, Lewis would have been unable to experience the joy she brought him in the moment. Unless he were willing to be grateful for this activator there literally would have been no Joy in his life. That *was* the deal!

It was Shelly's last night in the group. She is the former Marine nurse we met earlier whose 10-year-old son had recently been diagnosed with leukemia. Unbeknownst to the other group members and myself, Shelly was waiting that night for a page from the hospital where her father-in-law was dying of cancer.

Earlier in the session, when asked to summarize her experiences for one of the new members, she said, "When I first came into this group I was so angry. What got me here was that, about four months ago,

I learned that my 17-year-old drug-addicted son had relapsed. After all we had been through with him I just couldn't believe it! My husband and I have been married for 20 years now and we have a good marriage. When I got home from seeing my son in the hospital that night I just freaked out. I was screaming and crying in the front yard and my husband grabbed my arms and shook me. The neighbors saw what he was doing and called 911.

This group didn't help me with that problem, because there really was no problem between us. I just didn't know that it was going to help me with all the other problems that were right around the corner. I guess God must have known something I didn't. I'm so grateful for having had this experience.

Now we have come to the end of our journey together. The Preface ends with the sentence, "When the student is ready, the teacher will appear." My task was to start you down the path of learning, and then, along the way, to give you the tools necessary to complete the trip on your own. If you have stayed with me to this point, you now have those tools. God speed, dear friend, in your quest for the miracle of living *without* anger.

AFTERWORD

Life is difficult. This is a great truth, one of the greatest truths. It is a great truth because once we truly see this truth we transcend it.
The Road Less Traveled, *M. Scott Peck, M.D.*

The notion of transcendence runs throughout this book. It is my fundamental belief that we, as human beings, can transcend the limitations of our angry nature and achieve the personal peace that God has planned for each of us. The German philosopher Reinhold Niebuhr gave the world what we now know as the "Serenity Prayer":

> *God grant me the serenity*
> *to accept the things I cannot change,*
> *courage to change the things I can,*
> *and the wisdom to know the difference.*

I would like to believe that the ideas found in this book are consistent with this profound prayer. Congratulations to those of you who understand what this book is all about, and who strive to live according to this prayer, for you have granted yourself one of life's most precious gifts—the gift of serenity.

On page 107 I set up a scenario whereby I extend the middle finger of my left hand and then ask an audience member, toward whom the gesture is made, to tell me what the gesture means. By now you appreciate the fact that the gesture is meaningless! Whatever meaning it has is based on the meaning you give it. When I make this gesture toward Val, she smiles and says, "You're #1 in my book too, baby." Given that "meaning" does Val anger herself? Of course not. Clearly, however, there are meanings you can assign to that gesture that will result in you upsetting yourself greatly. The point to remember is that the meaning does not reside in the gesture, it resides in your head, and you are responsible for choosing one meaning as opposed to another.

FURTHER READINGS

Attenborough, Richard. *The Words of Gandhi*. New York, NY: Newmarket Press, 1996.

Beck, Aaron T. *Prisoners of Hate: The Cognitive Basis of Anger, Hostility, and Violence*. New York, NY: HarperCollins, 1999.

Bennett, William. *The Book of Virtues*. New York, NY: Simon & Schuster, 1993.

Bernard, Michael E. & DiGiuseppe, Raymond. *Inside Rational-Emotive Therapy: A Critical Appraisal of the Theory and Therapy of Albert Ellis*. New York, NY: Academic Press, 1989.

Covey, Stephen R. *The Seven Habits of Highly Effective People*. New York, NY: Simon & Schuster, 1989.

Ellis, Albert E. *Anger. How to Live with It and Without It*. New York, NY: Citadel Press, 1977.

Ellis, Albert E. & Dryden, Windy. *The Practice of Rational-Emotive Therapy*. New York, NY: Springer, 1987.

Hauck, Paul A. *The Three Faces of Love*. Philadelphia, PA.: The Westminster Press, 1984.

Janoff-Bulman, Ronnie. *Shattered Assumptions: Towards a New Psychology of Trauma*. New York, NY: The Free Press, 1992.

Kassinove, Howard (Ed.). *Anger Disorders: Definition, Diagnosis and Treatment*. London, Taylor & Francis, 1995.

Kushner, Harold S. *When Bad Things Happen to Good People.* New York, NY: Avon Books, 1981.

Lebell, Sharon. *The Art of Living: The Classic Manual on Virtue, Happiness, and Effectiveness.* New York, NY: HarperCollins, 1995.

Nottingham, Edgar J. *It's Not As Bad As It Seems: A Thinking Straight Approach to Happiness.* Memphis, TN: Castle Books, 1994.

Peck, M. Scott. *The Road Less Traveled.* New York, NY: Simon & Schuster, 1978.

Prager, Dennis. *Happiness Is a Serious Problem.* New York, NY: HarperCollins, 1998.

Stockdale, James Bond. *Courage Under Fire: Testing Epictetus's Doctrines in a Laboratory of Human Behavior.* Palo Alto, CA: The Hoover Institution, 1993.

Telushkin, Joseph. *The Book of Jewish Values: A Day to Day Guide to Ethical Living.* New York, NY: Bell Tower, 2000

ABOUT THE AUTHOR

Bradley P. Barris holds a doctorate in clinical psychology and is president of the consulting firm Barris & Associates Inc. Using proprietary Self-Management System programs, Barris & Associates has pioneered the development of seminars for mental health professionals, teachers, law enforcement personnel, attorneys and executives, providing them with psychological tools necessary to manage emotions and behaviors in the face of ever-greater personal and professional challenges.

His first book, *When Chicken Soup Isn't Enough: Managing Your Anger in an Increasingly Angry World*, has sold nationally and is available on audiotape through Recording for the Blind and Dyslexic. Businesses, Department of Veterans Affairs hospitals, individual U.S. Army, Air Force and Navy bases, private psychology practices, correctional facilities, schools and law enforcement agencies currently use the book. Employee Assistance Programs, including Owens Corning Corp., the Federal Bureau of Investigation office in Los Angeles, and the Johnson Space Center (NASA), also use the book.

Known for his uncompromising directness and use of humor, Dr. Barris appears regularly on radio and television discussing topics associated with anger and other aspect of psychology. He is a member of the prestigious National Speakers Association (NSA).

Suggestions for improving this work would be warmly welcomed. Address all correspondence to:

Bradley P. Barris, Ph.D.
5327 McKans Cove
Memphis, TN. 38120
(901) 830-8857

OR

E-mail address: *noangerdoc@aol.com*

OR

Visit our website at *www.noangerdoc.com*

"I've heard some of the greatest speakers in the nation, and Dr. Brad Barris is definitely among them!"

"I am in management with 50-plus people. These techniques will provide me with extra productive hours daily. What an amazing gift!"

"I attended your workshop in Corpus Christi. I am using the methods with a very angry and disappointed injured worker and he seems to be getting it. Thanks for your words of wisdom."

I have had a rough two years and I am always angry and I don't know why. I'm depressed with a huge black cloud hanging over my head. I would like to thank you. This has been full of insightful food for thought. Thank you for the great effort in your presentation, your style, and your information and for breaking through to me. It might have saved my life."

"Dr. Barris provided one of the best programs I can recall attending in years. The professional program content was practical, useful and humorous. Most of all Dr. Barris has the courage NOT to present disgusting, hypocritical Political Correctness. He is real, authentic and very, very refreshing."

"How do I thank you? I can't begin to tell you how much I enjoyed your seminar today in Irvine. I recently had major heart surgery and have been on a quest since then to resolve both the physiological and emotional problems that contributed to my overall condition. I have experienced extreme anger on different occasions all of my life, more often than not over many inconsequential situations. Your seminar and book (I bought six of them for my siblings) will help me deal with those situations in a positive manner in the future. You have already helped me immensely and for that I am forever grateful."

"After years of living angry, you have given me clear instructions to make my professional and personal life better. This is great. Why don't they teach this stuff in school?"

"This is the most amazing presentation I have ever seen. I have workable real tools to deal with the stress I feel about being a nurse in these 'entitled' times. The gift to me personally is even greater because you have given me the last piece of the puzzle to close the door on anger."

If you are interesting in learning more about the types of seminars offered by Barris & Associates, please write us at:

Barris & Associates, Inc.
5327 McKans Cove
Memphis, TN. 38120

Phone us at 901.830.8857,
Fax us at 901.763.3314,
or
visit our website at *www.noangerdoc.com*